An Agenda for Equity

Responding to the Needs of Diverse Learners

Searetha Smith-Collins

Published in partnership with the
American Association of School Administrators

ROWMAN & LITTLEFIELD EDUCATION

A division of
ROWMAN & LITTLEFIELD PUBLISHERS, INC.
Lanham • New York • Toronto • Plymouth, UK

Published in partnership with the American Association of School Administrators

Published by Rowman & Littlefield Education
A division of Rowman & Littlefield Publishers, Inc.
A wholly owned subsidiary of The Rowman & Littlefield Publishing Group, Inc.
4501 Forbes Boulevard, Suite 200, Lanham, Maryland 20706
http://www.rowmaneducation.com

Estover Road, Plymouth PL6 7PY, United Kingdom

British Library Cataloguing in Publication Information Available

Library of Congress Cataloging-in-Publication Data
Smith-Collins, Searetha.
  An agenda for equity : responding to the needs of diverse learners / Searetha Smith-Collins.
       p. cm.
  "Published in partnership with the American Association of School Administrators."
  Includes bibliographical references.
  ISBN 978-1-61048-723-8 (cloth : alk. paper) — ISBN 978-1-61048-724-5 (pbk. : alk. paper) — ISBN 978-1-61048-725-2 (electronic)
  1. Inclusive education—United States. 2. Response to intervention (Learning disabled children) 3. Educational equalization—United States. 4. Effective teaching—United States. 5. Academic achievement—United States. I. American Association of School Administrators. II. Title.
  LC1200.S65 2012
  379.2'60973—dc23   2011043227

Printed in the United States of America

Every learner will learn if given the background, experiences, and opportunities to succeed in a caring learning environment, organized to meet their needs by a dedicated, competent teacher. Every child deserves that.

Every teacher can help every child learn if given the background, experiences, and opportunities to succeed in a caring teaching environment, organized to meet their needs by a dedicated, competent leader. Every teacher and child deserves that.

Searetha Smith-Collins

Our greatest contribution is to be sure there is a teacher in every classroom who cares that every student, every day, learns and grows and feels like a real human being.

Donald O. Clifton

Contents

Preface   vii

Acknowledgments   xi

Introduction   1

1   Identifying the Need   9

2   Understanding the Need   21

3   A Glance into the "Regular" Classroom   31

4   Meeting the Need   39

5   The Black Male Agenda   57

6   Assessing the Outcomes   67

7   The Learning Target   71

8   Avoiding Internal Struggles and Pitfalls   85

9   Queries and Opportunities   93

10 Transitioning to Schools and Classrooms of the Future   101

11 Lessons Learned: Bringing Order to the Potential
    for Chaos   109

12 Meet the Kids   115

Appendix: A Comprehensive Curriculum/RtI Design Tool   123

References   139

About the Author   143

Preface

"Teachers, you are the shapers of thought and the molders of sentiment, not for this age and of this generation alone, but of the ages and generations to come. You are making history by those you teach . . . you are the few that are molding the masses." Reverend G. M. Elliott's words addressed to the Alabama State Teachers Association (ASTA) in 1888 typify the historical fervor of teachers' dedication to their work. Currently, we are in a time when the tenets of public education are being challenged.

What lessons have we learned and what do we need to consider for the fulfillment of the civil right to a democratic public education for American citizens? These issues are of special concern to Americans of color and low-income families whose children struggle to learn in the neediest schools. These students, as well as others, need a stronger approach and response for a more effective educational opportunity.

Justly, public schools now are being held accountable for the education of every child. Teachers are being asked to make reliable instructional decisions and provide authentication of measurable student learning. Difficulties surface when trying to manage data and accommodate appropriate instruction, especially for students who have learning difficulties and disabilities.

The purpose for writing this book is to shed more light on the complexities of teaching and learning, especially when executing justifiable change in education. The classroom improvement strategy known as Response to Intervention (RtI or RTI) models the intent of the book, which is threefold:

1. To help define decisive actions needed for identifying optimal ingredients that will ensure equity in student learning.
2. To clarify the need for appropriate responses to leading, teaching, learning, and providing intervening support for our most challenged students.

3. To contribute to educational dialogue with the hope and expectation of bringing a bit of order to the potential for chaos that seems to be permeating public education today.

Children as products of the educational process are like no other. First, they are not inanimate objects; they are subject to various feelings and responses to classroom and school changes and culture (norms, values, safety, care, personal and social interpersonal relations, and organizational structures). Also, they are "other people's" children who are heavily influenced by the people in their lives, which influences what happens to them. Children cannot be researched and developed with expected outcomes like inanimate objects.

Unlike software that can be experimented on over and over and then returned for lack of functionality, or a new car feature that does not catch on, or an idea or hunch that does not work, a child cannot be discarded or tucked away on a shelf marked "Rejected." If something goes wrong or an instructional year fails to produce results, the human child loses ground in learning in predictive ways. Society pays an extremely high price for educational miscalculations and miseducation. Options for outcomes span from education to incarceration, with the first being the more desirable choice.

Although we need to be more decisive in our actions and responses in public education, it appears that just about everyone thinks they know what to prescribe for the dilemma of public education. This is the case because education is not a defined profession, leaving it vulnerable and open to interpretations and inventive perceptions. In reality, we are talking about the growth and development of complicated, individual human beings and their ability to learn and develop in healthy ways. Although there are similarities, there are enormous individual and group variations and conditions that create both predictable and unpredictable responses to mainstream educational development and treatment.

The bulk of the writing in this book is new thinking, although some of the content was drawn from previous authored articles that formed a framework for reflection and current thought. It is somewhat amusing that the evolution of education has led back to many of the theories and research conclusions that were considered futuristic thinking twenty years ago. An example of this phenomenon will be discussed later in the book in a discussion about educational technology. It is intriguing to see proposed innovations from people with no educational experience or background to know what will or will not work in the complex world of schooling. If the innovation does not take hold, and most do not, the assumption is that change does not happen.

It takes having a variety of educational experiences across the spectrum of education levels and classrooms to fully understand what has potential and what has flaws when it comes to training and implementation for an idea. More important, it takes a great deal of understanding of the education landscape to know how to implement change so that teachers can master new ideas or tools. As a result, we have uneven accomplishments of various teachers in various schools who have the knowledge and skills to help students march toward the future. The teaching and learning agenda is the greatest educational challenge. What makes it difficult involves several elements:

1. Motivating student participation and involvement
2. Providing accommodations to which all learners are legally entitled
3. Teaching to differing learning styles, needs, and abilities
4. Providing powerful teaching and learning for all students based on accountability measures

Getting right to the heart of the matter are equity and discriminatory concerns related to the misidentification and overrepresentation of African Americans, Latinos, low-income students, and others, especially males, who are referred to and placed in special education programs. Drastic change is needed simply due to the fact that serious efforts of school improvement over time have not reaped sustained, large-scale positive achievement outcomes for the majority of challenged learners. There are implications for determining the extent to which current school improvement efforts align with preparation of leaders and teachers. Informing practice involves knowing what works and what does not work for all of the intricacies of today's learners.

Those who will find the information applicable are educators, school leaders, political and government officials, policymakers, state education officers, parents, community members, business and special interest groups, university and college professors, professional organizations, and others who are intricately interested in improvement of student learning and equitable conditions. Each stakeholder will find insights and conceptual views of how to facilitate the work of teachers and educational leaders who are focused on nurturing and educating all students in their care.

If collective powers can be marshaled in a common direction and maintained on behalf of educators, families, and students, perhaps all Americans will benefit from the educational profession and public school system as prescribed for a democracy.

Acknowledgments

There are many people who contributed to many of the thoughts throughout the writing of this book. It started years ago during graduate study at the University of Washington's School of Education in Seattle. Under the guidance of three critical professors, many of the undergirding philosophical views that were developed proved to be significant in the evolution of education over the past few decades. Dr. Richard Andrews, my caring advisor and expert in educational leadership, led my pathway into the School of Education and the School of Business, which allowed me to integrate both fields. Dr. James Banks, a guru in multicultural education, channeled my knowledge into understanding how multicultural perspectives and occurrences shape outcomes for diverse students. The late Dr. Kenneth Sirotnik helped me to understand the meaning of rigorous educational research.

To the many mentors, coaches, and colleagues who shared their knowledge and expertise throughout dynamic conversations, you are among the many contributors to this book. Irving Sato, an early pioneer and leading authority in gifted education, showed me how to marry rigorous and challenging, higher-level subject matter content for gifted and general education.

Over time, as a teacher, principal, executive school district leader, and businessperson in various decision-making roles, I learned that children do not come in neat little packages. It is a serious mission to provide truly equitable learning to improve life chances. Children come to school with the hope of having a successful learning experience. They also want to gain validation. Some children have to deal with real monsters outside the school doors, but still they come to learn in what may be the only caring, safe place they know.

I could not have written this book without spunky debate with my husband, Dr. Jacob Collins, whose insight and wisdom permeates the contents of the book. There are so many family, friends, and colleagues that I should mention, but I will just thank each and every one who has graced me with friendship, kindness, knowledge, and encouragement.

To my mother, Oleatha Green, who now does more observing than guiding, and my deceased father, Elbert Green, I carry the torch in your honor. Thank you for valuing education and ensuring that I, along with my two sisters, had the opportunities and wherewithal to compete when called upon to do so. To Qualin and Katanna, I am happy to see that you are preparing to take your place as the future generation of caring and competent people. I pass the torch to you.

To DaShaun and Michelle, thank you inspiring me to understand that achievement shows up at different times for different people in different ways. To Ginger, you wear the label "teacher" well. You could have chosen any profession, but you decided to continue the legacy as a committed, recognized outstanding teacher.

Finally, I dedicate this book to the loyal, committed educators who have responded to the highest challenge: to become a member of a profession with the title master teacher and exceptional leader.

Introduction

It's the challenge that confronts general education teachers everywhere: How can I know the right method to use with the right student, just in time to prevent school failure? A major question of the day is this: What is the most reliable technique for teaching students, and how can we achieve equity and best serve the needs of all children?

In the past, there was common vision and understanding of what schools should teach all students. Today, through innovation, creativity, and redefining the intent of public education, those standards and requirements span the universe in the name of new reform. Our job is to understand how to increase effectiveness with consideration for all aspects of a child's growth and development. Other important questions are how change can be managed and how desirable change can be accelerated.

These topics are of special concern to people who live in poverty, people of color, and those who do not have the same abilities as others to progress easily through the schooling process. Deep-seated effects of discriminatory practices remain persistent in society and American education. The indicators can be seen historically, economically, politically, and socially in school communities and society at large. Most specifically, we see the evidence of impact in the poorest neighborhoods, on Indian reservations, in the most disadvantaged families and schools, and in statistics such as imprisonment.

Schools have changed, and they will continue to change over time, especially when one considers teaching philosophies and methods. The new change is driven by national calls for increased proficiency standards for college and work readiness, new assessments to support those standards, more advanced content, and increased graduation standards. All of these changes are intended to ensure competencies necessary for the resourcefulness, competitiveness, and productivity of future Americans. Instead, there are unintended consequences based on the omission of three critical factors:

1. Policies and practices to support new requirements
2. Evidence to support the "know-how" for wide-scale implementation
3. Social and educational policy changes to ensure in- and out-of-school access and success for all

These are the areas in which educational transformation efforts fail.

The pendulum is once again swinging. We are searching for strategies to ensure success, and we are struggling to shift instructional methods to prepare all students for challenges to march toward the future. The optimum development of each child has come to the forefront with the aim of having children acquire as much knowledge as they can, as quickly as they can. Some cry out for more academics, rigor, and testing. Others demand that we put the brakes on a bit and refashion some of the approaches driving improvements in schools. I propose that we pause and examine ways of helping children learn and develop optimally.

While the national conversation centers on a common core and higher standards, there is a huge discrepancy in content offerings and capacity building in various public schools. Let's take a look at the current "College for All" and "Algebra for All" movements as a response to the call for increased rigor in student learning. Should all middle school students take algebra in grade 8 whether they are ready or not? What are the prerequisite critical thinking, abstract reasoning, and brain developmental and student and teacher requirements? What problem-solving skills are needed in addition to high-level content? How do you teach algebra to students who are five or six years behind their peers? How do you catch these students up in a short period of time so they can be prepared for three additional higher-level math courses? Is Algebra for All by eighth grade, or four years of higher-level math requirements for high school graduation, realistic on its own appeal?

The reality is that many secondary students are not prepared for the new mathematics learning standards and requirements. Certain building blocks and support systems must be put into place before students can board the "College and Work Ready" train. Let's play this out a bit more. What if all students were college ready and completed four years of college successfully? Since colleges and universities have quotas and preferred students who can be accommodated, what colleges could all students attend?

To probe a bit further, with the rising college costs, the lax economy, and the exorbitant cost of college already being beyond the reach of most middle- and low-income families, how will all students afford to go to college? How can all students avoid the debt of college if they graduate with huge college loans to repay over several years of their future life? These questions become especially pertinent at a time when many college graduates cannot find jobs in their major field or any other. Has the rhetoric been clearly thought through, with the appropriate policies and support put in place for long-term effects and access?

Also needing reexamination, in addition to academics, we want learners to develop the personal resources needed to strengthen, safeguard, and enhance their sense of worth, dignity, responsibility, and self-respect. At the same time, we want to encourage curiosity, compassion, and care for the environment and humankind. We want skills, but, equally important, we also want citizens with the personal assets needed for surviving in an interdependent society and world. Students need life skills to know how to navigate business, careers, the world, and family and personal living. When is a teacher to teach these skills?

Even though to some this might sound like twentieth-century philosophy, judging from what many high school graduates do not know and are unable to do, more knowledge is needed on how to manage a family, perform simple repair tasks when needed, have a better understanding of the meaning of good nutrition and wellness, and cook a meal beyond fast food, for goodness' sake! These are enduring daily living skills that people have needed and will need for years to come. These are the skills needed when technology breaks down or when problem solving or creative thinking are needed to handle a life situation dictated by events.

This is in no way intended to imply that children do not need twenty-first-century approaches to teaching and learning—that certainly is a must. Also, there is no intention to suggest that children should be sorted into treatment centers for the college ready versus the work ready. I simply mean that policy issues must be fully examined with balance and full understanding of the impact, consequences, and complications of implementation.

Because of the fast pace of life, these personal resource skills are taught neither in the school nor at home, and there is no common agreement in these areas. If we are talking about "all," we have to ensure that *all* students have access to equal information and developmental opportunities in all areas, including the ability to adapt and survive. The only place that learning by all can happen is in public schooling. This is why structured, organized public education processes and systems are needed—to ensure that all students receive the preparation required to succeed and thrive in society equitably. This can be accomplished in various ways.

Are we skipping over critical skills to get to a new age of higher-level knowledge? With the current trend of creating innovative public schools, do we have any idea what access to curriculum, teaching, and learning all students have? The intent to not to stifle creativity or local control or to separate students into tracks for higher-level and lower-level learning. The issue is that there are many combinations of skills and knowledge that American students must develop. We have to be more deliberate to define the meaning of a comprehensive education for all.

It is time to place the pendulum in balance and return to a common understanding, vision, and view of public education. For example, in the past, when college readiness and rigor were the buzzwords of the day, we increased Advanced Placement courses and eliminated teaching of practical skills. A case in point: A decade or so ago, high schools provided strong vocational/technical programs. In the rush to increase rigor, career vocational/technical education programs and courses were pretty much eliminated in many middle and high schools. You can find only remnants of those schools and programs today.

After reducing or eliminating most of the vocational departments and programs, especially in urban districts, now we find that, along with college readiness, there is a push to restore those programs to fulfill the need to provide for service and technical fields and career readiness as well. In our zealousness to move to a higher level, we did not anticipate future needs and shortages of high school graduates who could take advantage of lucrative workforce jobs and careers in the service and technical industry. So today,

> the graduation rate has reached its highest point in two decades. The proportion of public school students earning diplomas for the class of 2008 approached 72 percent, exceeding an earlier peak in 1991. Every racial and ethnic group posted solid gains for the second year of improvement. (Editorial Projects in Education Research Center, 2011)

However, there is a catch to the good news. Today, we find that there are certain jobs available for those graduates, but few Americans, including recent graduates, are skilled workers who are ready to fulfill technical and service jobs. We should define what knowledge and services are needed now and for the future and then provide equalized opportunity and support for both academic and applied priority areas. We have to decisively figure out how to help each student make steady progress to reach the finish line in both college and technical professions.

Public schools should not operate as special interests, public-private islands, or low-producing factories. Nor should they become special attractions for money-bearing entities that serve selective populations of students. Public education is about producing an effective education for every student who shows up. Public schooling in America should remain a system that continues to struggle with itself to revitalize educational opportunities. As one journeys through this book, there will be a blending of conceptual knowledge, research, and educational practice that broadens the view of the general education classroom.

There are many complexities that need to come together to determine how to integrate data with the precise instruction for each student. The real challenge is to ensure that all students have access to learning that can be called upon in various situations. There are several academic foundational skills missing from the march to the future for underperforming students:

1. Vocabulary, reading, and comprehension
2. Prior knowledge or background needed to navigate new content
3. Inability to recall information
4. Inability to think through, ask, or answer higher-level questions
5. Inability to respond to ambiguous questions or those with more than one answer
6. Cultural-biased attitudes, material, and assessments
7. Lack of having been taught the knowledge and skills
8. Lack of test-taking skills to demonstrate knowledge

These are the skills that commonly challenge rigor and access to advanced knowledge and thinking for struggling learners. It is essential that we take the time to understand how to increase the effectiveness of learning conditions that can help both teachers and students. We must offer a coherent vision for powerful and realistic content and instruction at every school level.

Again, it must be made clear that reference being made is about modifications and accommodations, not low-level expectations. Should children be provided a truly responsive educational experience with decisive support, their needs and academic goals might be more readily attained. The book is designed to help navigate some of the issues that are endemic to public schooling today and to delve a bit more into potential and future consequences.

The child is at the heart of the educational process. The K–12 school years are the most pertinent ones in a child's educational life. This is when the building blocks for future success are crystallized. The effects of school are accumulative. Decisions must be based on accumulative data that help define what approaches are best for individual students. The educational process should be genuinely adaptable and relevant. Unfortunately, schools in our nation treat different students differently. The dichotomy can be seen in schools for the "haves" (advantaged) and "have nots" (disadvantaged).

As in any high-performing organization that gets results, a portrait of what occurs in school systems and classrooms, in general, can provide an understanding of teaching and learning experiences:

- High-performing, successful schools and districts usually have large numbers of highly skilled, experienced, certified teachers with content expertise and multiple degrees.
- Children are exposed to a succession of more competent, highly skilled teachers in high-performing systems. In other words, a child has a greater chance of having "good" teachers in most grade levels and classrooms year after year than in low-performing systems.
- There are differences in knowledge and mastery of pedagogical processes (the ways teachers teach) and instructional and program accountability related to success as a content teacher.
- There are differences in the balance of theory and application necessary for various courses.
- There are differences in qualities needed for supervising teachers and in determining which practices and conditions are needed for teacher development.
- High-performing schools and systems develop and retain more high-quality teachers.
- Many of the conditions that exist in high-performing systems are not replicated in low-performing systems for various reasons.
- High-quality teachers who work in inner-city districts often do not remain because of adverse working conditions (e.g., not receiving a paycheck for months; not having workable technology, instructional supplies, or textbooks; concerns about safety; feelings of being unappreciated; etc.).
- High-performing systems generally have maintained facilities, supplied with instructional resources, including up-to-date, regularly maintained, and creatively used technology, science labs and equipment, and updated, well-resourced library/media centers.
- Regular attendance is maintained by teachers as well as students, and generally, in high-functioning school systems, students come to school prepared for the educational challenges ahead.
- High-performing school districts and schools usually have stable leadership and staffing.
- Teachers often have control over decisions in their classrooms. Most important, usually they have communities that support education (Smith-Collins & Collins, 2006).

When measuring high-performing schools and classrooms, it is puzzling why it is not clear that the positive attributes that exist in high-performing systems simply are missing or not represented in lower-performing systems. Yet the expectation exists that the attributes can be modified and low-performing schools can be brought to scale and achieve at the same level of measures as high-performing public or private schools.

Teacher quality, retention, and stability and effective student learning in low-performing systems are not a mystery when conditions such as the ones listed earlier are absent. This is not to excuse low performance, of course. Low-achieving schools should not be permitted for *any* child. They are not conducive to the future success of public education as a business (Smith-Collins & Collins, 2006). It is important to understand, however, that the ability to succeed is directly proportional to the breathing space and time allowed for instructional changes to be successful. School improvement takes on a unique connotation in the educational setting. Rather than sprinkle a little magic dust here and there, why not factor in structures, systems, protocols, support systems, and other elements that are needed to remove learning barriers and create functioning organizations?

Regardless of the seemingly insurmountable issues, only through examining and addressing the logical, historical, and evidence-based errors over time can we truly address equity and excellence. Responsive and inclusive schools and classrooms can be modified to provide opportunities for all to thrive. These are all major undertakings unto themselves. Nevertheless, as educators, we must engage in the process of education by asking the deep questions that lead to deeper levels of understanding about how to extend and adjust the principles and goals needed to prepare students for a successful society and world.

It is with this intent that we must critically and creatively focus on the roles, actions, and intended and potential unintended consequences ahead as we revisit forgotten solutions and stimulate healthy debate about proposed and new education solutions for school improvement.

Chapter 1 of this book identifies many of the unique needs of children in schools today. Response to Intervention, a current classroom improvement strategy, is used throughout as a framework for what it means to identify methods to help define and increase equitable opportunities for student learning. This chapter is guided by two queries:

1. What does it take to equip teachers to effectively teach "all"?
2. What does it take to help teachers put the pieces together systemically and individually?

Chapter 2 operationally and procedurally defines RtI with an interpretation of what roadblocks may stand in the way of success in the general education classroom. Chapter 3 provides snapshots of RtI in action in various settings to help explore a deeper understanding of the elements and responsibilities that are needed for successful implementation. Chapter 4 is an excerpt from a past article that is pertinent to the plight of black males and other youths who find themselves as outliers in the equity agenda.

Chapter 5 discusses some examples of where RtI has demonstrated its value and risks as an innovation. It also highlights national outcomes that have been produced in some of the more difficult arenas. Chapters 6 and 7 use curriculum as the centerpiece for judging the quality of content and equity in student learning. Chapter 8 pulls the optimum ingredients together to define what is required to implement an innovative strategy, such as designing systemic, comprehensive curriculum and RtI frameworks with critical content and understanding in mind. Questions and suggestions provide mediating factors for implementing RtI as a systemic initiative in chapter 9.

Often technologists will note that after a decade of innovation and millions of dollars spent on technology in schools, there is little to show for such efforts in most classrooms today. Chapter 10 discusses why a "means to a purpose" often fails to take hold in education, and why there is little impact on teaching and learning. Chapter 11 shares perspectives on what is needed to bring order to the potential for chaos in public education and details some specific practices that lead to increased student academic achievement that can be brought to bear. And final thoughts are offered in chapter 12, as the support for today's students and youth is presented as the focus of the work.

Someone once said, "Schools are perfectly designed to get the results they get." If that is true, perhaps through the analysis of RtI, as one transformation effort, there may be a chance for *real change* to take hold in the general classroom. Much will depend on what we have learned and endured over time. The rest may depend on understanding which principles should remain essential to the foundations of public education and which are worthy of drastic change. We are reminded of our charge:

> Dismayed by the present and frightened by the future, the people once again turn to their schools for answers. The demands of "minorities" for social justice have surfaced issues hidden too long. Full educational opportunity still eludes our grasp. . . . In these troubled times we need to stand back and look at our schools with attitudes of reason and objectivity. . . . The improvement of our schools is more than a worthy cause; it is essential for the survival of a democratic people. (author unknown)

Identifying the Need

If we were to compare a school system to a human body, each of us should be viewed as an individual cell or organ that keeps the organism alive, healthy, and functioning.

Cheryl Dales, Richmond City Public Schools Teacher of the Year, 1966

THE OPTIMAL MIX: RESPONDING TO THE NEEDS OF STUDENTS

Imagine a school where every teacher understands how to meet the needs of each child. Imagine each of those teachers using critical data for educational planning with the understanding of how to track and monitor individual student progress to put a plan in motion. Imagine that every teacher is committed to the progress of every student, and each one is inspired to learn at the appropriate level of understanding. Envision a school where learning for "high-risk" students is based on powerful prevention/intervention techniques that address individual strengths and weaknesses. Visualize what it would mean if all of these efforts could once and for all break the cycle of school failure.

For decades now, educators have undertaken collective efforts to determine how to improve student learning and structure equitable educational opportunities for all. Establishing the right mix of ingredients can have a powerful influence on teaching, learning, and school success. Accomplishing this goal, however, has not been overwhelmingly successful or scalable over time.

A great illustration of the problem is a third-grade student who had difficulty learning to read with proficiency, no matter what the teacher tried or was coached to do. The general education teacher, Ms. Jones, was in her third year of teaching and was recognized as one of the best teachers on staff. Nonetheless, this one child was very disconcerting. Each day, as Ms. Jones watched this child struggle to read, she came to the realization that she did not have adequate tools in her instructional toolbox to solve the problem or respond to this student.

As for most teachers, the image of failing to know how to teach a certain child was very disturbing for Ms. Jones. As a result of that experience, the following summer Ms. Jones enrolled in a Specific Learning Disabilities Fellows Program to learn how to diagnose and access learning difficulties and disabilities. She later enrolled in a graduate program specializing in developmental and remedial reading to become a reading specialist. One must seek support and self-identified professional development targeting areas of needed strength. One of the most critical roles of teaching is to build structures of knowledge that can strengthen proficient learning.

Many elements influence quality instruction and student achievement. Response to Intervention, commonly known as RtI—one of the popular educational buzzwords circulating today—seeks to promote best thinking on what teaching practices and interventions are working, and which are not working, for individual students. As a model of universal design, RtI integrates processes that uncover and make learning accessible to students who have learning differences. An additional aim is to guard against the possibility of misidentification of learning needs in the general education classroom (Burns & Ysseldyke, 2006).

A pivotal strategy undergirding the philosophy of Response to Intervention is to apply evidence-based interventions and strategic lessons, thus making it possible to influence the continuous progress for each student. As was learned by Ms. Jones, the third-grade teacher, preparation for teaching missed some very critical knowledge related to learning differences and disability:

- Using knowledge of high-quality instruction and interventions matched to individual student needs
- Understanding the impact of learning rate over time
- Unraveling how to make the precise important instructional decisions to maintain the learning continuum for all learners (Pierangelo & Giuliani, 2007)

When trying to capture the needs and challenges of students, efforts surround the following goals:

- Reducing or eliminating performance and achievement gaps
- Providing timely identification of prevention and intervention techniques
- Analyzing and using data efficiently for continuous improvement and progress

- Distinguishing between lack of appropriate instruction as opposed to learning differences and learning disabilities (National Joint Committee on Learning Disabilities, 2005)

Challenges surface when attempting to fit RtI seamlessly into classroom instruction and build capacity for efficient teaching and learning. If one were to take a glimpse into most of the nation's public school classrooms today, one would find many successful learners. However, a prevailing finding also would be that there is an absence of a solid, adaptable foundation and practice that is flexible enough to respond to various learner abilities and requirements. Glaring data indicates that despite their ability, far too many students are failing academically.

Educators are working against roadblocks that get in the way of successful learning experiences. Let's consider some of the conditions and serious threats to positive health, growth, and academic development that can trigger failure to learn in school. Imagine the classroom and educational impact on the following students:

- The child who misses several weeks of school and then returns with little or no explanation
- The three-year-old whose mother fails to pick her up at the end of the day
- The child who has been abused
- The child who has no clean clothes, food, dental care, or glasses
- The child whose parents have been killed
- The child who has been in several foster homes
- The eighteen-year-old ninth-grade student
- The gifted child who sits idle waiting for others to catch up
- The child who has attention deficit disorder or other handicapping conditions
- The super angry, misbehaving child who curses at teachers and has been suspended from school several times
- The unruly or unresponsive child
- The runaway or homeless child
- The child who speaks a first language other than English
- The shy, well-behaved, invisible child who is sure to go unnoticed

Several of these examples are real circumstances that were documented by Robert E. Pierre (2008) in the *Washington Post*. Others are situations that are the realities of many students who arrive at school every day. Children facing a court date or another new foster home can't focus on getting ready for a high-stakes test. Older students who have to stay home to help take care of younger siblings cannot focus effectively. Some have to work to help their family survive. Teenage parents often do not know how to fully develop and prepare their children for school and student learning.

In order to move all students forward, there must be a deep understanding of the root causes of underperformance. Issues include socioeconomic status, health and medical care, degree of poverty and family support, degree of development of background knowledge and understanding, school preparedness, vocabulary and literacy development, teacher preparation and quality, experience and expectations, and exposure to curriculum, instruction, and program offerings. All of this is coupled with the interrelationships of race, gender, ethnicity, culture, language, and abilities; the need for variation in frequency, duration, and intensity of instruction; and life situations and stressors.

It must also be said that risk factors should not profile a student. High-risk indicators can be predictive, but exposure to a risk factor does not automatically place a person in a category of learning differences and disabilities. Some students tend to have resiliency and skills, self-esteem, toughness, motivation, intellectual street smarts, family and extended community bonding and attachment, and protective and adaptive shields to help compensate for risk factors.

There were probably more students who had these capabilities in the past when families were more intact and parents and communities pooled resources to raise, support, monitor, care for, and shield children from high-risk factors. Today, we see more students who lack the provisions, protective shielding, and capabilities to thwart off risk factors, so the appropriate adults are critical to provide the appropriate preventative or intervening supports to students at risk of school failure.

One or more disparities can set the stage for a need for prevention and/or intervention services. Frequently, disparities are more pronounced in urban inner cities and in rural areas. Deficiency areas on tests and assessments often reveal that students are not functioning at the expected or tested grade or course level. The disparities can also be root causes for barriers to alertness, attention, behavior, language readiness, visual or auditory problems, or other handicapping conditions. The major task is for teachers to determine if a student is not achieving due to poor instruction, a learning difference, an environmental stress or experience, or a disability.

A *learning difference* has to do with developmental time or ways that individuals learn. A *learning disability* has more to do with a disorder or handicapping condition that creates a disparity between potential and actual performance or demonstrated ability. In any case, the whole child must be considered in terms of strengths, weaknesses, and individual differences, and needs must be identified and strengthened.

As demonstrated earlier by Ms. Jones, who struggled to help a child learn to read, general educators are not generally prepared to identify the nature of the problem of struggling learners. A collaborative effort must be made with the help of special educators, related service providers (psychologists, speech and language teachers, specialists, etc.), and general classroom teachers.

As one current trend, RtI appears to be promising for special-needs and other students who require explicit or specialized expertise and interventions. Also, it appears useful for students who have limited opportunities for success in school and for those who fall off the pathway to successful student achievement. The difficulty is to figure out how to overcome the many hurdles that get in the way of helping every child learn effectively.

FROM PARTS TO WHOLE: UNDERLYING NOTIONS

There are significant principles of learning that are fundamental to education and school transformation:

1. The early childhood years are powerful times for building foundations for human learned intelligence.
2. Usually the early years are most effective for providing commanding prevention and intervention.
3. Parenting can be the most demanding task that we undertake.
4. Some children do not have the benefit of rewarding parents and at-home support.
5. Learning is demanding, and it can be one of the most gratifying or frustrating experiences for a child.
6. Children can accommodate information and learning that falls within their capabilities to process, grasp, and internalize it (Piaget, 1954).

Several underlying assumptions shape the desire for wholesome child educational growth and development. If these basic ingredients are in place when a child starts school, a school is ready to educate its students:

1. Children need to be properly nourished, be secure in their home lives, and receive supervision and guidance from caring adults.
2. Young children—in fact, all children—have to feel loved and wanted. If those feelings are not optimal, children perceive that they do not matter to others.
3. Every child has to have adequate self-esteem (self-worth).

4. Children need to have adult role models who help them acquire positive qualities such as honesty, kindness, the love of learning, compassion for others, and acceptance of differences, including people, thoughts, and beliefs.

Educators are confronted with myriad factors attributed to learning problems and disabilities as they try to figure out how to provide the best education for every child. As noted earlier, children's problems originate from a variety of intervening factors that are manifested in different ways across classrooms and schools. Educators must determine which combination of strategies and programs best counteract the relevant societal inequities. Also, they must intervene in student behavior that often camouflages root causes.

In 1982, the late Ron Edmonds, founder of the Effective Schools Movement, published a paper titled "Programs of School Improvement: An Overview," which stated a part of the Effective Schools mantra that is not often reported: "While schools may be primarily responsible for whether or not students function adequately in school, the family is probably most critical in determining whether or not students flourish in school" (Edmonds, 1982).

In addition to recovering academic skills gaps and synthesizing new knowledge and skills, children must develop and grow emotionally. They must learn to manage feelings, values, motivation, behavior, and attitudes. It is well known that many students are vulnerable to poverty and negative in- and out-of-school risks. As a result, many students have difficulty in school. Often they are assigned a multitude of labels: disadvantaged, alienated, at-risk, high-risk, troubled, difficult, struggling, vulnerable, angry, discouraged, disengaged, disruptive, troubled, and so on. All of these descriptors imply that many come to public schools with a great number of barriers that can impede teaching and learning. If ignored, these challenges become classroom management or behavior and learning problems, which often become reasons for emotionally disturbed and learning disabilities special education referrals.

When children are hungry, ill, unhealthy, uncooperative, or not self-managed or self-disciplined, they cannot effectively perform. "Teachers are being asked to be social workers, disciplinarians, police officers [and solvers of the ills of society], as well as teach. With this expectation, there is no way that teachers can be successful in any of these roles, especially that of teacher! It is no coincidence that the students with the highest suspension, expulsion and arrest rates have the lowest scores in reading, math, writing, and the lowest graduation rates." (Jackson, 2010, p. 1)

In many public school classrooms, the school day is spent on control rather than instruction. The truth is, schooling cannot take place in disparate parts, and teachers cannot solve the entire learning equation for all students. Long-standing research validates that children develop along multiple, interconnected domains that collectively influence learning. A "whole-child," student-centered, broad-based response calls for interventions that are appropriate for the developmental stage of children. This includes tackling proficiencies in mental skills and knowledge (cognitive); growth in feelings, emotions, attitudes, and behavior (affective); and sensory and motor skills to fully address why a student is struggling. In- and out-of-school policies, politics, and provisions must reflect a comprehensive, integrated vision of how to appropriately respond to the diversity of student and family needs.

Adverse experiences affect the intensity and emotional quality of engaging and carrying out learning activities. "Children often become discouraged, which results in passivity, lack of effort, giving up easily, acting out, boredom, depression, disengagement, anxiousness, anger, withdrawal from learning opportunities, or even rebelliousness towards teachers and classmates" (Skinner & Belmont, 1993, p. 572). It is not a matter of excuses or blame—it is about acknowledging challenges and making provisions for in- and out-of-school barriers.

Many schools and districts are adopting and implementing Response to Intervention in hopes of pinpointing effective identification of learning needs so that strategic teaching can be provided. The focus of RtI is general education teachers; however, they may not be the best answer or resource for students who have severe problems. Special educators and specialists are needed upfront to assist as behavior specialists who can help deescalate certain behaviors when students become overly defiant angry or volatile. Although roles and responsibilities may change within a new process, other clinical and content specialists must stand ready to assist, such as reading, literacy, and mathematics coaches and specialists, as well as student service workers who can help mediate and facilitate changes in the general classroom. Schools must serve as conduits for bringing together resources and channels for addressing whole-child needs. If applied early enough and continued as needed throughout childhood, interventions can be effective as critical factors in student learning.

REVISITING PAST PRACTICE

Although it is yet another revolution for the general classroom teacher as the primary source of lesson delivery, the task is more challenging today than ever. Attempts to individualize instruction, mainstream and include special-needs students, coteach, team-teach, and integrate instruction have occurred in the past. Now teachers must fast-forward to seek new ways to deliver instruction to students.

They must understand research-based principles and assemble and construct appropriate combinations of cognitive processes with prevention and intervention procedures. This must be accomplished while matching processes to curriculum, teaching techniques, assessments, and resources, including technologies to capture the interest of today's digitally passionate students. All this has to be done at the earliest point to respond to the most critical needs when anticipated.

Current data suggests that many general classroom experiences result in underperformance, underachievement, misidentification, overrepresentation of learning needs, and disproportionate numbers of students (mainly African American, Latino, male, and low-income) being placed in certain disability categories in special programs. Some of the most abused areas are those for the learning disabled, autistic, emotionally disturbed, and those with behavior disorders. According to the Council of Exceptional Education and the National Alliance of Black School Educators (2002), many students are at high risk due to several practices:

- Failure of schools to educate students from diverse backgrounds
- Misidentification of learning needs and use of tests
- Ineffective match of instruction to student needs
- Insufficient resources
- Less well-trained teachers who make learning more difficult
- Limited ways to adequately inform the effectiveness and impact of instruction on student learning
- Lack of sensitivity to differences in learning ability, culture, language, and environmental dynamics
- Lack of collaborative planning and involvement of parents/guardians and students in the intervention referral process

In response, RtI sets out to lead to a more precise understanding of how to apply additional knowledge and skills to better anticipate and broaden options for learning and achievement. A concern, however, is that there has not been sufficient time to engage in the professional inquiry necessary to address RtI and all the challenges faced in the general classroom. Many teachers remain a bit hesitant because little objective research has been documented as evidence of success for many educational innovations. Nevertheless, the teeth behind RtI are federal mandates and civil rights laws that are influencing decisions, such as the following:

- The Individuals with Disabilities Education Act (IDEA, 1977), which protects the rights of students with disabilities to have access to an equitable, free, and appropriate education.
- The Individuals with Disabilities Education Improvement Act (IDEIA, 2004), which allows the use of 15 percent of allocated funds for alternative ways to identify students with disabilities.
- The No Child Left Behind Act (NCLB, 2001), which tracks educational progress of groups of students in schools and districts.

All of these mandates have increased the role and involvement of general education classroom teachers in the special education intervention process. In addition, general education teachers are being called upon to provide evidence of success and results for all students, inclusive of answers to such questions as those listed below:

- Are all students included and engaged?
- Are classroom management issues reduced?
- Are fewer students referred for special education services?
- Is student achievement improving and measurable, including students who struggle in school?

Providing intervention services for underperforming students is not a new endeavor. In the past, when these laws were enacted, other theories of intervention and prevention existed as part of the educational reform agenda. Initiatives were implemented to address low achievement, the impact of high poverty, achievement gaps, overidentification, overrepresentation, and the education of students of color, mainly African Americans, as compared to the progress of their white counterparts.

Some of the intervention programs were funded by the U.S. Department of Education Elementary and Secondary Education Act. Others were funded by Title 1, which addresses reading, mathematics, parent involvement, and compensation for the impact of poverty; Title 8 (dropout prevention); Reading First (evidence-based early reading techniques); and Head Start, Even Start, and other early education programs that focused on parenting, early education, and combating poverty. Strategies of the past were programs for three- and four-year-olds, individualization, criterion-referenced testing, continuous progress, early reading development, and computer-assisted instruction. All had a goal of intervening in student learning to increase success in school.

Most of the reforms did not provide sufficient ways to increase teacher proficiencies or to increase scale and sustainability. In the area of special education, federal law increased the role of general education in the development of individualized education plans (IEPs). Although general education teachers are charged with inclusion and mainstreaming students in the least restrictive environment, many do not feel they have the instructional time and expertise to increase complexity or to compact curriculum to streamline or modify learning for low- or high-ability learners.

It is still common practice for many teachers to refer students to a reading, math, or other specialist or to refer a struggling learner for evaluation by a psychologist for special education eligibility. This practice contributes to backlogs for referral decisions, overrepresentation, and misidentification in special education. Also, this accounts for some of the high dropout and low graduation rates that remain in many public schools. This is especially true for those who come from poor socioeconomic conditions.

To put it simply, the majority of educators feel overwhelmed. Full understanding and implementation of RtI remains ambiguous to most. Regardless, the needs of struggling learners and the risk to schools remain enormous. Jim Marshall (2007–2008, p. 28), former CEO of SpectrumK12 School Solutions, Inc., expressed it this way: "Doctors tell us those chronic illnesses such as cancer, HIV or osteoporosis have the best outcomes when they are detected early, or better yet, prevented. Why aren't we practicing what we preach?"

First, we must look at the context of educational change. Then we must consider the history or success of the many changes in public education over time. Very critical to RtI as a change strategy are complications spurred by the varying interpretations and understandings. For example:

1. How will RtI bring quality to overall instructional efforts?
2. How will value be added to the proper mix of challenge, support, encouragement, and personalized learning to help students operate around learning challenges?
3. How can teachers manage the processes and procedures and make RtI work in the regular classroom?
4. Can teachers develop the skills to truly provide differentiated and strength-based teaching for every child?

Efforts often are hampered by a great deal of organizational fragmentation in public schools that hampers student and staff learning. Suggestions and recipes have not provided a coherent menu of techniques. Some solutions involve a dash of smaller class sizes, longer days and school years, parent involvement, school takeovers, common core standards, prescribed curriculum and instruction, new technologies, and so on. Such isolated approaches often promote a lack of focus or interruption to program integration.

Classroom teachers are faced with this backdrop as they are asked to explore yet another improvement initiative. This is not to say that there is not a need to address instructional improvement in general and public education. There is common agreement that there is a wide variance in teacher abilities that account for most of the differences in student test scores. However, there is not much more than ephemeral agreement on "how . . . and what steps—must be taken to see that every student has access to high quality, responsive teaching" (Berry, Hoke, & Hirsch, 2004).

Solely focusing on strategies that intervene in student academic learning and behavior in the general classroom will yield limited results if total school conditions are not aligned in support of high achievement (Ortiz, 2001). Instructional decisions must be based on school-wide principles that are compatible with RtI, such as the following:

1. Learning problems must be identified early and accurately.
2. Learning problems must be addressed through a consistent, reliable approach.
3. Evidence-based, high-quality instruction must be matched to individual student needs (National Joint Committee on Learning Disabilities, 2005).

Effective instruction involves sorting through complex learning tasks for the optimal components that separate reasons for discrepancies in learning. Sometimes, programs address the wrong need or involve ineffective procedures. Public education has a history of seeking ways, both inside and outside of the education system, to more aggressively support the education of children, especially those born into poverty. Most of all, public education must find its way back to purposeful, meaningful systemic reform that is focused on agreed-upon core policies and strategies that allow educators to stay on course without distractions.

CHAPTER 2

Understanding the Need

Experience is what causes people to make new mistakes instead of old ones!

Anonymous

DELVING DEEPER INTO RESPONSE TO INTERVENTION

Like solving a puzzle, it is important to have a clearer understanding of what an improvement strategy such as Response to Intervention is and what it does. As opposed to trial and error, RtI uses levels of problem-solving approaches to identify and understand which programs and practices are most effective for a particular child. Proponents of RtI suggest that diagnosis and treatment of learning needs can be managed in the general classroom as the first point of contact. Special education referrals would be managed through a problem-solving, pyramid-type tiered intervention approach.

Although considered by many as a new method for responding to the strengths and weaknesses of learners, RtI was used in the past decade as the School-wide Positive Behavior Support (SWPBS) process. It also has been used to identify students with specific learning disabilities (SLD), now commonly known as learning disabilities (LD). The methods were challenged for limitations in measuring intelligence for students from diverse cultures and languages, so the focus of RtI was expanded (National Joint Committee on Learning Disabilities, 2005).

The reauthorization of the Individuals with Disabilities Education Act of 2004 called for a different way to determine special education eligibility. At the same time, the U.S. Department of Education Elementary and Secondary Education Act of 2004 developed requirements for using research-based reading programs and reading intervention services. As a result, RtI expanded to determine whether a lack of appropriate developmental reading instruction was taking place in the general classroom.

Other variables, such as progress monitoring and problem solving, became significant to the process based on past research that indicated potential for improved student outcomes. Over the past few years, the focus broadened to investigating different variables that were added based on past research on assessment practices, cultural and environmental data, early identification, intervention services, and student performance in the general classroom.

Through evidence-based instruction and laser-like data, RtI grew with the expectation that:

1. students with varied learning needs would be better served in the general classroom; and
2. the numbers of students who were misidentified or improperly placed for special education services would decrease.

As required by IDEA for identification and eligibility for learning disabilities, validation must be documented for the following:

1. Early intervention services
2. Tiered intensities for academic and behavior interventions
3. Screening, progress monitoring, and data collection
4. Collaborative team problem solving and decision-making
5. Documentation of appropriate general classroom core instruction, and fidelity to implementation of interventions prior to referral

Interventions of various types must offer personalized or small-group assistance based on the student's area(s) of weakness.

RTI FRAMEWORKS

When students do not respond to core instruction or specific interventions designed to meet their needs, the most prevalent problem-solving approach used is the Multitiered Prevention Model. This model provides instruction on core curriculum, providing extra support to identify when help is needed for individual students. As with the other models, it applies the best available evidence on how to teach core content.

Use of this model requires strong, sustained teacher skills and knowledge on how to implement a learning plan using tiers. Individual tests are administered when students fall below the 25th percentile on standardized tests (Sugai, Horner, & Gresham, 2002). Students are monitored for satisfactory progress measured against average benchmarks, then placed in a pyramid of three levels of intensity for instruction and interventions.

1. *Tier 1:* Instructional strategies are usually flexible groupings with specific techniques for various learners in class, after school, or during extended day sessions. Classroom teachers teach the core lessons with the support of others. Interventions are administered by the teacher, volunteers, paraprofessionals, or tutors who work under the guidance of the teacher. The ideal outcome is to serve the majority (80–90 percent) of students successfully. The theory is that the bulk of the class should be served successfully. No more than 10–15 percent of students should need further assistance.

2. *Tier 2:* This tier involves more strategic instruction and interventions for students (the 10–15 percent referred to above). Additional diagnostic tests, monitoring learning several times per week, and collaboration with the intervention team is required for progress review and appropriateness of instruction. Interventions may involve core curriculum and supplementary programs to reinforce skills. Parents/guardians should be involved in the process at this level.

3. *Tier 3:* The most intensive level is intended for the lowest 5–10 percent of students who have the most need. More frequent intervention based on specific assessments should be provided. Personalized instruction is delivered based on diagnosed needs. If students are unsuccessful, documentation of evidence often leads to a special education referral. All, including parents and students, have an active role in the intervention process at this level.

All RtI models involve *universal screening* to identify areas of strengths and weaknesses of students in classrooms. *Progress monitoring* tracks whether or not interventions and instruction are working. For example, at Tier 1, after teaching a specific intervention for decimals, students should be assessed every six weeks to determine mastery. Complications in determining progress might include inconsistent methods or timeframes, lack of attendance, or life-altering events such as divorce in the family during significant instructional periods. If learning is not taking place, individual *frequent diagnostic assessments* are administered. *Fidelity assurance and evaluation* of the process defines the degree of reliability and consistency of classroom instruction and student results.

ADOPTION TRENDS

RtI is being implemented in various degrees in various school districts across the nation. The size of a school district matters. For example, in large urban or rural schools, there could be large numbers of students who require interventions, creating difficult management and tracking problems for teachers. A small rural district or school may not have adequate resources to provide appropriate services and offerings. In any event, RtI should be systemic, as opposed to being implemented in isolated classrooms.

Because Response to Intervention as described above is relatively new, it is not clear how to effectively apply it or to apply the process in varied contexts for specific purposes. For instance, there is no consensus on whether or not RtI should become a part of the identification process for students with disabilities.

Teachers have found that RtI is not easy to implement at the school or classroom level. Starting in 2007–2011, a district survey has been implemented by GlobalScholar and SpectrumK12 School Solutions. Several partnering organizations are involved, including the Council of Administrators of Special Education (CASE), American Association of School Administrators (AASA), National Association of State Directors of Special Education (NASDSE), and RTI Action Network.

The four-year study was administered to gauge how widely RtI is being adopted in the United States and what obstacles early adopters are facing. Data for the 2011–2012 school year has been analyzed from 1,390 nationwide respondents and identifies critical trends over previous years (2007–2010).

THE FINDINGS

The SpectrumK12 School Solutions study found that RtI implementation has been increasing steadily, with 68 percent of the respondents indicating full or in-process district-wide implementation. This is up from 60 percent in previous years, when it was reported that districts were either piloting RtI, in the process of district-wide implementation, or already implementing it districtwide. While the trend is moving upward, only 24 percent of the schools have reached full implementation with fidelity. Districts with 10,000 or more students were more likely to have fully implemented RtI than smaller districts.

A significant number of responding district administrators reported that RtI adoptions were quickly increasing across grades and school levels. Slightly more than half of the districts had a formal RtI implementation plan in 2011, which is up from 48 percent in 2010. In 2009, 71 percent of the districts were involved in adoptions, up from 44 percent in 2008. In 2011, reading remained the dominant content area for initiatives, followed by mathematics and behavior.

Each year, the most popular starting point was the primary level—kindergarten through grade 3. In 2011, 80 percent of the respondents reported that RtI was being implemented with fidelity in one or more areas of reading, writing, mathematics, behavior, or science. Academics remained ahead of behavior, mainly in areas of screening, assessments, research-based interventions, and data-driven decision-making.

In 2009, the greatest increase in adoptions was at the high school level, mainly targeting ninth and tenth graders (National High School Center, National Center on Response to Intervention, & Center on Instruction, 2010). Implementation in secondary schools was more complex, because elementary models were not useful for scaling up what was needed in secondary schools. In the SpectrumK12 study, similarities across adoptions at all levels included a focus on reading, mathematics, and then behavior, with reading progressing more smoothly than the other subject areas. This may largely be due to the availability of more identified research-based interventions for reading.

Other reports noted that RtI adoption rates were lower at the middle and high school levels due to such reasons as the following:

1. Teachers not understanding how to effectively serve secondary school students
2. Perceptions that RtI is an elementary school initiative
3. Complications of teaching with fidelity across 56 periods or 150 students per day
4. More subject matter complications
5. The need for more identified reading and teaching strategies for unprepared students

Other accounts concur that RtI models are beginning to provide more behavioral supports and interventions for English-language learners (ELL) at all levels. RtI is implemented differently across functions and settings in different states and regions. Some are deeply immersed in systemic initiatives. Others use an integrated approach to strengthen and reward increased student achievement. Several are just starting to think about adopting RtI. Still others have decided to bypass RtI for whole-school reform initiatives encouraged by competitive federal grants, such as the current federal school improvement initiative, Race to the Top (RTTT).

Most schools employ RtI frameworks using assessments for universal screening and tiered levels for mastery and intensity of interventions. Instructional decision-making processes were commonly used to determine the course of action for individual learning plans, small-group and individual instruction, and ongoing assessments. Progress monitoring for tracking fidelity to instruction and intervention was commonly found in most RtI school efforts. As of 2011, most districts have school-based leadership teams in place at the school level rather than the district level.

Most of the districts have a unified effort between special education and general education staff. If the efforts are coming from a single area, it was reported that general education teachers were more likely to lead. A new finding for the SpectrumK12 study in 2011 was that a higher percentage of staff is now trained in RtI as compared to previous years, at least at the overview of the RtI process level. The most common areas are in core curriculum and differentiation of instruction. The study has identified consistent barriers to adoption and implementation; in descending order, these are as follows:

1. Insufficient teacher training
2. Lack of intervention resources
3. Lack of resources for instruction
4. Instruction and/or progress monitoring
5. Lack of data and knowledge for implementing and charting student performance

Sufficient data is still needed to determine the impact of RtI on annual yearly progress (AYP). "In respondent districts that had sufficient data to determine the impact of RTI, 76% indicated improvement in achieving Adequate Yearly Progress targets (AYP) versus 24% who indicated that AYP had not been met" (SpectrumK12 School Solutions, 2010).

Sixty-two percent of the schools were beginning to create personalized instruction for all students in 2011, which was up from 49 percent in 2010. Districts reported about the same level of data on referrals to special education; five in ten districts have data, and eight in ten of those reported reductions. In previous years, 87 percent indicated reductions in the number of student referrals for special education services. In 2011, new data reported that a small percentage (14 percent) of the districts indicated that legal proceedings or official complaints have steadily grown.

In previous years, funding sources—including the Individuals with Disabilities Education Improvement Act of 2004, the No Child Left Behind Act of 2001, the American Recovery and Reinvestment Act of 2009, and RTTT funds—provided more than $4.35 billion in federal money for RtI initiatives. Additional sources were grants, general districts, and Title 1 and IDEA Early Intervening Services funds (SpectrumK12 School Solutions, 2010). With current spending pressures in most school districts, concerns for continued funding have gained increased emphasis.

To clarify the common understanding of the meaning of "full implementation," findings were based on the following practices in the SpectrumK12 School Solutions (2011) study:

- Universal screening in each participating building at least three times a year
- Implementation of a validated core curriculum in reading for all students
- Instruction and interventions organized in a multitiered system for supports
- Use of clear decision rules to move students between tiers of instruction
- Evidence-based intensive instruction (in addition to core and supplemental) to students who need it based on data
- Progress monitored using technically adequate measures at least weekly for students with intense learning needs
- Progress monitored using technically adequate measures at least two times per month for students with supplemental learning needs

THE PROMISE OF RTI

Data tells most of the story about the strengths, weaknesses, and needs for instructional decisions—in other words, data talks. Conversely, one must have the aptitude to translate the meaning of data to determine if more information is needed to paint a complete picture. To illustrate the point, in 1971, Senator Walter Mondale expressed apprehension about data to the American Psychological Association. Concerned about the array of research and research-based programs and offerings that were supposed to provide clear policy options, Mondale expressed the limitations and complications of cumulative and systemic research:

> What I have not learned is what we should do about these problems. . . . For every study, statistical or theoretical, that contains a proposed solution or recommendation, there is always another equally well-documented study, challenging the assumptions or conclusions of the first. No one seems to agree with anyone else's approach, but more distressing: no one seems to know what works. . . . As a result I must confess I stand with my colleague confused and often disheartened. (Hunter & Schmidt, 1996, pp. 324–25)

Although there is little comprehensive research or data readily available to help understand the impact of RtI in actual practice (especially in large-scale initiatives), there are promising signs. Matthew Burns and James Ysseldyke (2006) examined four large-scale implementations of RtI: the Heartland Agency Model in Iowa (Heartland), Ohio's Intervention-Based Assessment (IBA), Pennsylvania's Instructional Support Team (IST), and the Minneapolis (Minnesota) Public Schools' Problem-Solving Model (PSM). The study was a follow-up to a collection of integrated studies of large-scale models. Questions and findings were as follows:

1. *Are there validated intervention models and measures to assure instructional validity? Findings:* Research consistently supported: (a) formative assessment, (b) frequent progress monitoring, and (c) informal assessment relevant to curriculum aspects of RtI. Instruction and effective interventions inclusive of these components were necessary ingredients for improving student achievement.
2. *Are there adequately trained personnel to implement an RtI model? Findings:* Training appeared to be an important component if implemented in phases that involved broad training. This was a critical component for preparation of general education teachers and other specified staff. It was projected that it would require a period of four to almost ten years for staff to achieve mastery of the process. Multidisciplinary collaborative teams were included in the training, but there was no consensus as to which professionals should make up the RtI response team.
3. *What leadership is needed to make RtI successful? Findings:* The Heartland and IBA emphasized local autonomy. Only IBA and IST required principal involvement. Therefore, questions about leadership remain unanswered. For example, should leadership come from special education, general education, or both? How much autonomy should building administrators have within their local schools? What should be the involvement of state-level departments?
4. *When should due process begin? Findings:* The length of time between parental referrals and completion of an evaluation plan is guided by federal and state mandates. IST has a time limit of fifty school days of instructional support and teacher involvement. Heartland and PSM provided "due process" protections in the final phases, which leaves questions about stages possibly exceeding state mandates for special education consideration. More research was suggested for placing timelines on the process to alleviate due process concerns.
5. *Is inadequate response to intervention a defensible end point? Findings:* The strongest defensible end point requires (a) accurate identification of the deficits responsible for lack of responsiveness to interventions within tiers; (b) data sufficiently valid to warrant the classification of LD, and

(c) evidence of positive or negative outcomes that are justifiable enough to classify students as responsive or unresponsive. More collective data was needed to support the findings of each approach, and the overall effectiveness of large-scale RtI models (Burns & Ysseldyke, 2006).

A need was suggested for overall research to determine the impact of RtI on various school populations. For example, it would be beneficial to know the effects of RtI on ELL students and the results and improvements for emotional behaviors over time. More clarity was needed to determine the relationships of RtI for several distinctions:

1. Success rates at each grade level or movement between tiers
2. Numbers of students who receive interventions beyond the primary level or move between tiers
3. Varied achievement measures (i.e., norms, benchmarks), and how progress is measured and used at the local, state, and national levels
4. Cultural and language contingencies and variability across contexts
5. Validity of interventions with various student populations in various settings
6. Knowledge of how fidelity is measured across complex school contexts and identification of teacher development models that are mindful of culture and equity

Other suggestions call for more complex views of the relationship of curriculum and Tier 1–level interventions. Also, the issue of perception and dynamics of culture, learning, and competence was suggested as a researchable focus. Illustrations are to map various data sources or to use school dimensions such as rules, interactions, background experiences, or cultural knowledge base (Artiles, 2007). Chrys Dougherty (2010) suggested the need for additional study of

- learners who enter school with large preparation gaps, especially at the high school level;
- instructional decisions on which strategies are best for accelerating academically unprepared students; and
- informing general education and response team decisions about which combinations of interventions are best for increasing student achievement as opposed to searching for a "magic bullet."

The bottom line is that data must be gathered and interpreted on important ingredients for measuring how well different populations of students learn.

CHAPTER 3

A Glance into the "Regular" Classroom

It is easier to know what to do than to do it.

African proverb

Response to Intervention has been presented "first and foremost" as the responsibility of general education teachers. It must be acknowledged, however, that when teachers serve large numbers of high-risk students with mixed abilities and varied challenges, it becomes very difficult to meet the needs of all students. The first step is for general educators to help rule out poor teaching as the major cause, which is often omitted.

We know that some schools manage to effectively educate all of their students. Each school represents a unique mix of teacher and student competencies, attitudes, and social, cultural, and political conditions and relationships. The combination of these dynamics influence how teachers relate and interact with students and how individual teachers demonstrate improved classroom practice. Typically, general classrooms were designed to serve students without disabilities. Inclusion was designed to ensure that certain children with disabilities could have appropriate educational experiences in general education. The general classroom teacher was a part of the team to ensure that experiences in other programs with specialists were consistent with those in class.

Because of this existing design, some general education teachers do not fully understand how to identify and employ successful teaching strategies for all the vast differences in learning needs. Others employ low-level lessons and expectations for certain students, or teach the same lesson in the same way for all students. In the name of educational reform, successful interventions are sometimes abandoned and replaced with the latest fad that passes through schools and classrooms.

Many general educators find it difficult to incorporate and master multiple strategies and assessments. Others have difficulty documenting and using data to objectively explain lack of student performance, progress, and concerns. Another weak link is that principal leadership is insufficient to provide persuasive influence or instructional guidance to build a school's capacity to effectively educate all students.

Newmann, King, and Youngs (2000) suggest five aspects for school capacity-building that are needed for making the shift to new roles and responsibilities in the general classroom:

1. Teacher knowledge, skills, and dispositions (including subject matter)
2. Pedagogy and expectations
3. Professional learning and community
4. Program coherence
5. Technical resources

In addition to effective principal or teacher leadership, even greater elements must be integrated into capacity-building in underperforming schools:

- Effective approaches to school and classroom challenges and behavior
- Practices and resources that demonstrate sustained student growth
- Time for teachers to think about what is being done and how to do it better
- "Know-how"—knowing what works with what students, when and where it works best, and under what circumstances, using what resources

SHARPENING THE FOCUS

Clearly, classroom teachers and school leaders are pivotal in determining academic student success; therefore, *preparation matters*. Again, as illustrated in the introduction in the recounting of Ms. Jones, the third-grade teacher, preservice development does not prepare most teachers for the wide variety of learning needs in today's classrooms. People frequently declare that "RtI is just what good teachers do naturally." There is a lot of truth in that statement; however, it is also misleading.

A teacher can be a "good" one and orchestrate positive results, but may not be utilizing the RtI model to reap these results. Master teachers and others have successful practices that should not be stifled in the name of RtI. For example, after Ms. Jones engaged in special training in specific learning disabilities, this added another dimension to her already effective teaching. The greater number of classroom teachers usually are prepared as generalists and may not feel confident about responding to the effects of trauma, serious behavior, or motor and sensory processing disorders.

Teachers and school leaders are challenged to provide the most suitable approaches for closing learning gaps or providing safety nets for all learners. This brings to the forefront a focus on university and alternative education teacher preparation programs. Through matching student outcomes with certain teacher preparation programs, school and university leaders must better identify which processes and university or alternative preparation programs are most effective for developing skilled teachers and leaders.

Along with strong preparation, teachers need a unique repertoire of strategies and resources to provide for personal, social, cultural, and academic needs. There are classroom and organizational structures that get in the way of systemic academic progress. Shortages of experienced teachers and teachers of color are problematic.

Educators in underperforming schools, especially in urban districts, often are deemed ineffective or not fully supported. Often teachers are caught in a web of multiple get-tough, "do it now or else" reform mandates. Sometimes this phenomenon creates cultural and racial dissonance for teachers and leaders of color. Feelings of alienation often develop when these educators are not in agreement with the promotion of new reform techniques or intervention initiatives. This happens when programs and strategies are not in sync with historical or cultural interests or when there are tensions with processes and the cultural practices that have been in place over time.

In frustration, many of these teachers who are strong, experienced educators are dismissed or leave the profession. This is a loss to students, schools, families, and the communities they serve. Other teachers are drowning in multiple initiatives and administrative, societal, and family duties, such as breakfast and lunch duty, meeting after meeting, recess duty, after-school programs, paperwork, homework detail, or other duties unrelated to classroom instruction. Federal and state policymakers, leaders, parents, and other stakeholders must address problems that are driving good teachers out of the profession.

Acceptance of new models such as RtI creates hesitation because of the perception that special education duties such as an overabundance of legal procedures, forms, and excessive paperwork are being shifted to the already full load in the general education classroom. Many special education teachers are perceived as being frustrated with Individuals with Disabilities Education Act compliance needs and requirements.

Some parents feel that general education teachers may not know which programs are best for their child's special needs. Others have concerns that individualized education plans (IEPs) and individual learning plans (ILPs) are not in sync. Legal challenges and lawsuits plague special education. There are exceedingly burdensome IEP compliance procedures that get in the way of teaching and learning.

Lesson design is another factor. Struggling students need support beyond core subjects. Therefore, if a student is failing algebra in the eighth or ninth grade, a specific intervention is needed to address a concept or basic skill through the RtI process. A well-thought-out RtI process and robust in-service and professional development programs can allay some of these fears and concerns.

If RtI is to be successful as a general classroom initiative, these issues will need to be addressed in the planning process before adoption or implementation. Professional development is important, but multiple workshops and training sessions that involve multiple topics can be another barrier. Teachers cannot process new curriculum, new resources, assessments, instructional strategies, programs, adoptions, and various technologies simultaneously. Classroom interruptions, cumbersome appraisal processes, lack of district/school priorities, and insufficient teacher support can make RtI implementations more difficult.

TEACHER ASSESSMENT

To provide clarity, it is important to emphasize that strong leadership, teaching, school improvement, and accountability are needed for better student outcomes. As in most professions, ineffective people must be identified, remediated, or removed through due process as quickly as possible. If the following are true, the teachers must clearly be evaluated and removed for the good of the students:

- teachers cannot embrace sensible, strategic change or innovations;
- teachers are weak in traditional or special education instruction;
- teachers do not show improvement after concerted effort to strengthen skills;
- teachers exhibit inappropriate behavior regarding the safety of students in any way that is not defensible;
- teachers are proven to impede teacher effectiveness and student progress; or
- difficulties persist in the implementation of new techniques after considerable training.

Matching teacher performance to student outcomes is one of the most debated topics in education today. RtI is not the place for this issue to land, however. Although some school districts have decided to mix RtI and teacher evaluation, it is not recommended, especially while RtI is in its initial developmental stages. When considering changing teacher attitudes and developing positive classroom improvement, clear lines must be drawn separating issues of development from appraisal. This becomes a crucial concern when judging appropriateness and fidelity of instruction and interventions.

In the RtI process, school leaders observe teacher performance for targeted subject area content. Peers, curriculum supervisors, or content specialists also observe, using checklists to provide feedback. Teachers can self-report regarding time on task and fidelity of effort. Teacher effectiveness based solely on tests and implementation of new instructional procedures and processes initially should not be used to judge merit or provide monetary reward for student achievement. This stance is taken because individuals enter learning in developmental stages, and there are several other considerations that must be examined:

1. Assessments and tests are prone to subjectivity and inaccuracies.
2. There is a lack of understanding about data and its interpretations.
3. There is a lack of ways to effectively and objectively monitor fidelity of implementation.
4. Knowledge of developing systems for evaluating and integrating effective structures for professional development and research-based interventions are lacking.
5. Sufficient structures and assessments for evaluating academic, social/ emotional, and behavioral interventions for all subgroups need to be conclusively identified.

Beyond educational assessment problems, staff capacity must be developed to synthesize data from multiple sources. Data management and analysis are time consuming and easier said than done, as noted by educational researcher Wesley Boykin (2010, p. 1):

> The lack of performance on any educational assessment tool in schools, especially those with challenging student populations, does not alone indicate failure. On the other hand, the adoption of a "value-added" performance appraisal model does not indicate that one is now making a decision in the best interest of children. The average person, including educators, has limited understanding of value-added systems, growth models, and other multivariate statistical techniques

that are being thrown around by politicians and their constituents. . . . [These assessment and evaluation tools] never had the intended use of identifying professionals who should be fired or awarded with additional pay.

Leaders and teachers have to understand what is happening to cause breakdowns in teaching and learning processes. This is where teacher evaluation must start. Criteria can be based on consistent difficulties in reliably making accurate conclusions for consistent planning and instruction. A teacher's experience level matters for every school year of a child's educational experience. Inexperienced or ill-prepared teachers who lack a cultural framework or background to work with culturally or linguistically different students may run into problems that warrant an evaluative response. It must be remembered that many of these tasks are challenging for even the best of teachers. However, the operative idea is that when there is consistent documentation of problems in the same or similar areas after efforts to help the teacher improve, action must be taken.

LEADERSHIP MATTERS

This is where the potential of leadership comes into the picture. In the role of instructional leader and resource, district leaders and school principals must understand these challenges and have the preparation and ability to provide support and strategic responses to the staff needs. Time is required for teachers to develop. Scheduling and related services must be given consideration, especially in matters related to motivation and offering students comprehensive learning experiences, within the scheme of RtI and intervention programs.

Principals and teachers must be able to master school programs and instruction without prejudice and bias. Educators, innovators, and other stakeholders must be thoughtful about issues of equity. Some of the practices that raise concerns are shown below:

- Innovations or programs with overreaching promises or diminished access to balanced school practices.
- Narrowing the curriculum to reading, writing, and mathematics, with little time for other interests or needs.
- Excessive focus on structured academics for young children (elimination of recess, play, and socialization time).
- Limitation or omission of physical education, health, art, music, science, social studies, electives, and extracurricular activities from the curriculum.

No matter how well intentioned, there is little to support the effectiveness of some current-day reform practices. There is little to no understanding of the long-term effects on learning or the children who are affected by the changes. Class and race differences surface when instructional and intervention programs create very different offerings and opportunities compared with those offered as balanced, "quality" educational experiences for middle- and upper-class students.

All of these concerns, challenges, and issues surround RtI. Assurances must be made for policies, procedures, and practices that are supportive of students and teachers, no matter the circumstances. Identification and best measures for predicting learning success and aligning RtI goals with organizational expectations are critical to the process.

CHAPTER 4

Meeting the Need

Fishing in deep water requires skill.

African proverb

PROMISING PRACTICES

Promising practices or activities are the elements or activities that distinguish successful efforts from less successful ones. Snapshots are just a brief depiction or part of the entire picture of what happens in an endeavor. To make sense of the features and interconnectedness of the practices, they must be considered in the context of the greater school system or organizational structure. Because most of the practices for RtI have focused on the elementary level, the following snapshots will highlight some of the more far-reaching RtI implementations that are taking place in a variety of settings.

SNAPSHOT: MY GIG: "MY GOAL IS GRADUATION"

According to the report *Diplomas Count 2011*, "The nation's public schools will generate about 145,000 fewer dropouts than the previous year," yet 1.2 million students remain who will fail to earn a diploma (Editorial Projects in Education Research Center, 2011). This data implies that while progress is being made, a great deal of work remains to impact the high school completion rate.

Response to Intervention is being used to help students who are likely to leave or have already left high school for a variety of reasons. Some are students who are overage or have personal struggles. Others have come to detours or potholes in the road to graduation. Logical strategies that are being implemented to address these students are providing pathways to acquire missing credits for multiple classes; providing transitions for ninth and tenth graders by structuring coteaching between English teachers and intervention specialists; offering Tier 2 instruction during study hall; and involving students in designing Tier 2 interventions (National High School Center, National Center on Response to Intervention, & Center on Instruction, 2010).

Often high school students are very capable, but for a variety of reasons the learning continuum has been disrupted, causing gaps in knowledge and skills. Sometimes, there are perceived gaps between where students are and where they need to be. In any event, for these students, high school completion seems insurmountable. Graduation does not seem to be within reach, so many make the decision to abandon their high school education.

Visualize disenfranchised, overage, underperforming high school students who are ninth, tenth, and twelfth graders sitting in one high-tech, workplace-like classroom. These are students who often are disruptive, turned off, disengaged, or truant from traditional classrooms. The students are orderly and busily working on individual learning plans leading to the goal of graduation. "My GIG" ("My Goal Is Graduation") is part of an individual learning plan (ILP) for mapping a path to high school completion, monitored by both students and staff.

Whether at Locke High School in Los Angeles, or several other sites in California, Maryland, Alaska, Michigan, or the District of Columbia, AdvancePath academies can be found in action. In each setting, AdvancePath academies serve approximately 120 students in groups of 60 per session. Realizing that high school students learn in different ways in different settings, this nontraditional intervention is a Tier 2– or 3–type, whole-child, RtI-like model. The intervention plan aims to reengage students in the educational process.

AdvancePath academies are not experimental. They were designed around longtime, research-based, recuperative methodologies. The secret sauce is the intervention design that strategically integrates best research and practices for alternative education and school dropout and high-risk learners.

Designers of the intervention did what most master teachers do without naming it: RtI. They applied many critical preventative and intervention methods that have been documented over time. The defining difference is the clever way the pieces were woven together to achieve optimum results. As a last stop for this struggling youth population, some of the carefully combined evidenced practices are the following:

- Integrated curriculum and mastery learning are core and aligned with the district's learning standards, the state exit test, and graduation requirements.

- The Northwest Evaluation Association (NWEA) Measures of Academic Progress are administered upon entry for universal screening, placement, curriculum planning, and academic growth.
- Personalized or individual learning plans are modified for each student at his or her instructional level.
- Instructional methods used include direct instruction, computer-assisted instruction, individual and small group, teacher facilitation, and individualized learning.
- A learning management system collects and produces manageable tracking data for continuous progress, including attendance, pacing, and rate of learning.
- Individualized education plans (IEPs) are integrated with the ILPs and graduation plans.
- Coordinated student services are monitored through an integrated process, which is a criterion often omitted in high schools.
- Learning and interventions are directed at literacy, personal development, course-taking, and preparation and postsecondary transitions.
- A safe, organized learning environment models responsibility for one's own learning.
- Clear parameters for student behavior, respect, and responsibility are a must.
- Teacher-student relationships are the most defining factor.

Certified school district teachers and staff are cooperatively selected and retrained in the academy methodologies. A blended model of "high tech, high touch" is used for curriculum and instructional delivery. Teachers use varied teaching modes matched to interventions, accommodations, and supplemental resources that are determined to best suit the need. Teachers and staff serve in multiple roles as case manager, mentors, coaches, facilitators, and guides.

Various pathways are used to meet the students where they are. Some are just a bit off track, and others are not motivated to complete their course of study. Some were frustrated with the pace of instruction and did not find school relevant or responsive. Others cannot see the light at the end of the tunnel, so they just give up. Several missed a great deal of school and retrieval options to get back on track. Still others had so many challenges in life that school was not their first priority at the time.

The staffing model includes a lead teacher and three other core-content teachers who jointly manage a shared caseload of students. A registrar/technical support person, special education teacher, instructional aide, and community liaison are involved, if included in a district's customized model. The academy is regulated for quality assurance by the school principal or designee and a staff person from AdvancePath. As partners, they collaboratively determine support levels for fidelity to the model and make decisions about professional development, student progress, instructional, and operational problem solving.

ELEMENTS AT WORK

AdvancePath staff understand these students and their problems. They are trained to help them focus on getting a high school diploma as a first step to restructuring life chances. Differentiated interventions that have proven to be most powerful are as follows:

1. Foundational core skills and competencies matched to course-taking at the student's reading level
2. A self-paced environment organized around extended, flexible timing
3. Pacing along with Web-based curriculum combined with textbook and other multimedia materials
4. Adjusting learning goals based on mastery tests that are administered at any time
5. Accommodating below-level students with audio and support for the content, scripted and highlighted text, chunking and scaffolding of text to center attention on specific concepts, and having the ability to have content read as a component of the curriculum

Youth and young adults learn how to become *students*. They receive instruction on how to develop study habits, organizational skills, and social responsibility through the use of study guides, note taking, and journals. This provides a way to capture and organize information needed for quizzes, finals, and end-of-course exams. All of this is done in real time, where students can boost and gauge their own progress toward the end point. They learn necessary skills to complete required courses and earn Carnegie units needed to complete requirements through rigorous content. Staff members provide individual and group support, attendance monitoring, and coaching for life skills. Students develop trust, confidence, persistence, and other citizenship and intelligent behaviors in preparation for transition to postsecondary, work, and life endeavors.

AdvancePath academy courses are matched to the particular district's and school's course of study. Students are enrolled in two self-regulated courses at a time. Classes can be scheduled in half-day (four-hour) or six-hour sessions in the morning, afternoon, or evening, depending on the district plan. The learning schedule is flexible enough to accommodate in- and out-of-school needs, such as work, family responsibilities, teen parenting, legal issues, childcare, and so forth. Coursework can be completed in school or at any time out of school. Tests and assessments are completed under the supervision of a teacher in class before the student can progress to the next unit or course. Operating on a year-round schedule, students can graduate at any time during the year, including summer sessions.

Interventions for social/emotional and behavior include teacher- and student-developed behavior plans, counseling, special education services, social skills development, home/community support, and time on task. As expected, interventions in these areas are challenging; however, teachers manage to successfully change patterns of attitudes, behavior, and attendance for the majority of students. Other components of special note are listed below:

1. A "school-within-a-school" learning environment where students feel ownership for a positive classroom culture
2. Frequent parent/guardian and student interaction and immediate feedback, benchmarking and sharing milestones, accomplishments, and concerns
3. Diagnostic preassessment and preteaching before each lesson and unit of study
4. Enrichment and accelerated learning
5. Professional development and ongoing team support specific to interventions and data analysis

Participation in the academy is based on school, dropout retrieval, teacher, caseworker, advocate, parent/guardian, or self-referral, or simply the need for an alternative or accelerated approach to learning or high school completion. Intake procedures involve interviews, completion of an autobiography, reviews, and verification of student transcripts. There is a reconciliation of credit attainment records and other pertinent school data by school counselors and the lead teacher. Program observation, student/family conferences, agreements, and commitments for procedures, course requirements, and participation are contracted.

Usually located on a high school campus, themes vary from a transitional academy (overage students for 6½ hours daily with 120 students) to a stand-alone or partnered academy (3- to 4-hour sessions or optional maximum of 180 students) to an independent academy (6½-hour day, up to 180 students) to a special education Tier 3–4 academy.

For instance, Dundalk High School in Baltimore County, Maryland, has a morning session and an evening session beginning at 6:00 p.m. that accommodates students who come from all over Baltimore County. This academy was customized to serve as an after-school offering. Students come to complete courses needed for graduation, make up missed coursework, take a required course that did not fit into a busy schedule during the regular school day, or accelerate a graduation plan. Students report that they often find it is easier to negotiate the pace of curriculum and complete course requirements more quickly with a higher level of understanding.

Data has surfaced that interventions are closing achievement gaps between black and white students, especially males. An example of the impact is provided by one of the many underperforming schools that incorporated the academy as a school improvement strategy. As a result of the implementation with fidelity, the high school was removed from the state's "watch list" the first and every year since the academy has been in place. The school district attributed its significant improvement in meeting graduation requirement targets to accomplishments of the academy. In addition, the number of students who passed the state's required high school exit exam significantly improved, which increased the school's pass rate as well as the number of students who completed high school with a diploma.

Another evolving outcome is the impact on closing the "discipline gap" that is closely connected to the achievement gap related to African American and Latino students, especially males. Through employing various techniques, including resiliency building, team teaching and learning, and a culture of trust and mutual respect created by implementing the Positive Behavioral Reinforcement Model (PBRM), the academies are proving to be optimal environments for providing students the opportunity to learn and graduate. The PBRM is one of the main reasons that behavior incidents dropped dramatically during the first six months students spent in an AdvancePath Academy, as compared to before their arrival. In one district, the AdvancePath Academy students collectively had over 250 behavior incidents in the six months prior to entering the academy as compared to only ten in their first full year in the academy.

SNAPSHOT: NATIONAL/STATE PREK–12 NETWORK

State and school district leaders are critical to the plan for implementing and reducing the complexities of RtI. The Positive Behavioral Interventions and Supports (PBIS) is a national, state, district, and school-wide resource for RtI. Serving prekindergarten through grade 12, the PBIS model uses the three-tier approach for planning, designing, and providing professional preparation for RtI implementation. Established around 2005, the network facilitates the following:

- Development of academic and behavior intervention systems
- Support for the integration of initiatives and practices for building a positive school and classroom climate
- Identification of appropriate prevention strategies
- Addressing consistency and coordination of effort using data across states and school districts

Member teams agree to define social expectations across all settings (classroom and nonclassroom). They develop plans to teach, review, and reward social expectations and establish clear and consistent plans for responding to inappropriate behavior. Network members employ data-based decision-making and establish programs for students needing greater support and engage family and community in schools (Washington State PBIS, 2009). In 2008, PBIS consisted of thirty-one state leadership teams, representing more than 8,000 schools and 46 states and Washington, D.C., with the greatest number of schools (805) in Illinois (Billingsly, 2009).

In 2009–2010, the Washington State PBIS Network involved 205 state teams that planned and shared experiences on models and lessons learned across RtI adoptions. Some of the successes of the WSPBIS are shown below:

- Reductions of 20–60 percent in office discipline referrals; for example, in 2005, Highline Elementary School District in Washington State had 1,286 office discipline referrals, but after four years of PBIS, this was decreased to 189, representing a gain of 165 hours of academic time recovered
- Reductions in suspensions/expulsions and dropout rates
- Reductions in referrals to special education for emotional/behavioral disabilities
- Increased instructional time and academic gains
- Increased school safety
- Increases in reported staff and parent satisfaction

SNAPSHOT: A SCHOOL DISTRICT

Using PBIS strategies, the Seattle Public School District developed procedures and protocols for adopting a RtI initiative at the district level. RtI was the vehicle used to obtain buy-in to the district's five-year strategic reform and state-mandated student achievement improvement efforts titled Excellence for All. The initiative was structured to facilitate three strategic goals:

1. Develop system and school capacity to respond to student needs before failure occurs

2. Integrate data-driven decision-making into instructional planning and reflection
3. Redefine and align processes and outcomes for coaching across disciplines (Billingsly, 2009)

A multitiered framework provided academic and behavior supports that defined levels of intensities for student intervention:

- *Tier 1* (universal at the classroom level)
  - Universal screening, high-quality instruction, and behavior supports for all students in the general classroom.
  - Interventions for universal academic and social/emotional classroom assessments.
  - Common planning time for staff in reading and mathematics and provision of text materials at the students' instructional level.
  - Provision of comprehension toolkits for teacher use and structures and techniques for explicit instruction of skills in strategic small groups.
  - Progress checks on targeted students.
  - *Examples of interventions* are (1) instruction for common school rules; (2) acknowledging and meeting school expectations and classroom rules aligned with school policies and rules; (3) targeted activities focused on attendance, truancy, inappropriate social skills, aggression, and disruptive behavior; and (4) teaching respect and bullying prevention.
- *Tier 2* (strategic level)
  - Targeted prevention/interventions for students who are identified as academically lagging behind grade level and educational setting.
  - Academic interventions, including small-group instruction in addition to core instruction, reading fluency development, extended-day homework assistance, or work in a computer lab.
  - Required extended time of at least sixty minutes after school for six weeks.
  - Instructional assistants work with the core group, the classroom teacher works with small groups, and in-class tutors work with math and reading interventions.
  - *Examples of interventions* are (1) small-group counseling, (2) Recess Club, (3) check-in/check-out, (4) social skills follow-along, and (5) bullying prevention programs, all dealing with inappropriate social skills and more intense disruptive behavior.
- *Tier 3* (intensive level)
  - Heightened, individualized interventions for students who are unresponsive to Tier 2 prescribed interventions.

o Academic interventions for groups of one to three students receiving additional instruction in core content.
o A district-directed math or reading specialist or coach assigned to provide one-to-one support.
o Behavior supports for students who received six or more office discipline referrals.
o *Examples of supports* are (1) a system questionnaire for behavior disorders, inappropriate social skills, disruptive behavior, aggression, bullying, withdrawal, noncompliance, and truancy and (2) a functional behavior assessment and developing an individual behavior improvement plan (BIP), along with individual counseling when prescribed.

THE PILOT

The Seattle schools used a pilot process to develop implementation protocols. Five schools and one volunteer site were identified to participate in the initial implementation. The Seattle version of RtI considered whole-child environmental, behavioral, and health factors as they applied to academic difficulties. Universal components that were implemented by each pilot school involved the following:

1. *Problem solving/collaboration* using a team approach, in which four critical questions were addressed:
   - Is there a problem? (problem identification)
   - *Why* is there a problem? (problem analysis)
   - What are we going to do? (implementation)
   - Did the plan work? (evaluation)
2. *Planning*, designing, and evaluation.
3. *Integration of data management:* School-wide screening, research-based progress monitoring, data collection, documentation formats for decision-making, and identification of student's performance goals and aim points.
4. *Staffing and support:* Leadership providing professional development; staffing resources; incorporating early and frequent communication regarding school failure; school improvement team (SIT) problem-solving team meetings; active roles in determining interventions, development of plans, and clear roles for implementing intervention plans. *Central Office services and support* included:
   - Facilitating stakeholder meetings for principals and senior leadership, parents, community groups, and advisory teams
   - Providing extra pay for facilitator participation and assistance to RtI teams

- Providing additional nurses and counselors
- Providing facilitator assistance and access to a university consultant
- Providing intervention screener kits (one per school), intervention guide books, SIT assistance, RtI manuals and documents, summer training, and ongoing professional development
5. *Parent involvement:* Early and frequent communication regarding school challenges/failure; involvement in SIT problem-solving team meetings, an active role in determining interventions and plans, and clarified roles during implementation.

Pilot school principals identified coordinators to spend two days per week on RtI implementation. The pilot schools incorporated components of RtI in their school improvement plans, completed an RtI self-assessment, and developed a SIT process. They also implemented and summarized data from the NWEA MAP, which focuses on mathematics and reading/language arts literacy. Three to five positive behavioral expectations were established for students, determinations were made for how to increase parental/family involvement, and principals identified potential resources for intervention support.

INDICATORS OF SUCCESS

Midyear MAP and end-of-year assessments of the pilot schools showed significant trends in both content areas. However, an independent audit of the pilot and year 1 implementation revealed issues that need to be considered before going to scale district-wide, including two shown below:

1. The district had a strong overview of an RtI model to pilot school teams.
2. Significant growth and headway were made in RtI implementation, which provided a pathway and jump start for helping other schools initiate the process. For example, the Franklin High School pilot team used data extensively for implementing RtI behavior interventions (Billingsly, 2009).

Other findings dealt with the actual "how-to" that needed additional attention for district-wide implementation. Follow-through recommendations made from an independent district evaluation of first-year efforts included the following:

1. A focus on RtI was needed daily, and a system-wide design was needed for consistent tiered academic and behavioral interventions.
2. A district-wide coordinator was suggested for implementation of the large-scale model.
3. Funding sources needed to be identified to help stabilize the initiative for long-term school support.

4. Year 2 implementation plans considerations were as follows:
- The RtI process needed to be embedded into the infrastructure of schools.
- More focus needed to be placed on academics.
- Student data systems needed to be aligned to RtI.
- The core program and instruction needed to be strengthened.
- Student data needed to be used for quick and accurate decision-making.
- Resource allocation needed to be determined for time, teachers, space, and materials.
- Cultural and linguistic needs beyond the awareness level needed to be addressed.
- Professional development needed to be embedded in the structuring of tiers.
- Communication for the district's vision to close the achievement gap could be improved (Billingsly, 2009).

As the Seattle Public School District approached year 2 of its RtI implementation, fourteen targeted schools were to administer the School Evaluation Tool and the Closing the Achievement Gap Benchmark Assessment. Targeted measures were fidelity to interventions, the effectiveness of the multitiered interventions, and determination of the level of assistance needed for improvement in the school. Wanda Billingsly (2010), former director of systemic intervention in the Seattle schools, indicated that RtI was providing the structure and framework for central office initiatives. Also, support systems for schools were being provided, as opposed to schools having to individually figure out how to piece together the initiative.

> We can all agree that all children deserve quality education in a safe learning environment with appropriately trained staff. What you will see is that this model does not require implementing all new procedures. It is more about integration of current research-based best practices (we are already doing) to be more efficient and effective in meeting student needs, and the good news is, it also keeps us in compliance with all of these at the same time. (Billingsly, 2010)

SNAPSHOT: SUPPORT FOR SOCIAL/EMOTIONAL DEVELOPMENT

Since 2008, Bailey Elementary School in Providence, Rhode Island, has operated a "full-service" community school serving 350 students. As a neighborhood hub for families, agencies work closely with Bailey to serve the needs for housing, health care, adult literacy, and a network of other out-of-school "wraparound" social services. As noted by Rebecca Box, the program director of an adult literacy center in Providence, "The goal is to increase academic achievement by providing family support." In some cases, family and student services are located in the school building, allowing the availability of community services from 6:00 to 8:00 p.m. "Perhaps if a teacher finds a child slipping in school and traces the root cause to homelessness, help can be found right down the hall where a social worker can be brought into the intervention process to help the family find temporary housing, thus helping the child to remain stable in the same school" (Borg, 2010).

As an urban school populated with many students who come to school with out-of-school challenges, the intervention strategies were built into the structure and organization of the school day. Children typically arrive at 6:00 a.m., are served a healthy breakfast, and have their homework checked by people who run a YMCA program. While students are in class, parents engage in adult literacy classes or visit their child's classroom. Parents of preschool children can take classes to coach them on how to prepare children for school and provide high-quality learning activities at home. In another part of the school, case managers from the John Hope Settlement House help parents find housing or jobs.

At the end of the school day, 120 children get extra help from their classroom teachers, who run the after-school educational program that is seamlessly connected to what is taught in the classroom. Another after-school program option allows children to choose from selected activities such as gardening, karate, or dance.

In 2010, Bailey Elementary was one of seven schools statewide (the only Providence public school) that made adequate yearly progress. The school was removed from the state Department of Education's Sanction List. Bailey educators are convinced that the wraparound social services helped the school meet more than twenty academic targets two years in a row. As an observer wrote:

> The power of this intervention model demonstrates how schools can be transformed to address the intervention needs of both students and families. In 2010, more than 150 children and families watched, as Bailey held a graduation ceremony for a group of adults who received literacy diplomas. There is no better result than to model the value of education. (Borg, 2010)

SNAPSHOT: RTI AND GIFTED EDUCATION

Precautions must be taken for RtI not to omit the needs of advanced or gifted learners. Students who have highly advanced or superior intellectual abilities or talents require developmentally appropriate learning as well. The RtI process can be adapted to include acceleration and response to the needs of advanced learners. These students perform or are capable of performing far beyond the norm of their peers. Their identifiable strengths and needs often are less emphasized or ignored. When addressing equitable learning, school districts must respond to all students, even those who are proficient and beyond.

Specific definitions and determinations should be made for potential and actual aptitude, academic ability, and maturity. Gifted education appears to be involved in a paradigm shift resulting in the drastic removal of gifted and honors programs in some school districts. Educational reform efforts must not leave these students out of the recipe for improvement.

Similar to the philosophy of inclusion for special education students, the trend is to teach gifted students in heterogonous (mixed-ability) general classrooms so as not to segregate or isolate learners. The idea is that brain and mind sharing will help all students achieve through group performance and group projects where everyone can benefit from the gifts and talents, interpersonal and team interactions and skills, and social development. Although the notion is very well intentioned, there are times that highly advanced students need to work and synergize and work in common, on critical or creative problems, goals, or projects, with other highly advanced students. It must be acknowledged that some students think and perform far above the skills and abilities of their teachers and peers.

Their questions, curiosities, thinking, and mental abilities can often far exceed the norm. While these students can spend some time in the general classroom, most of the spectrum of highly capable students' needs cannot be met in heterogeneous general education classrooms. Although this is an unpopular philosophy in some circles, support for heterogeneous groupings in the general classroom calls for ability clustering or above-grade-level placements for students who are far ahead of peers.

These students grasp concepts quickly, deal with complexities and problem-solving content and dilemmas with logic and evidence, can be independent workers with the need for only a little facilitation, and often require varied levels of lessons, extensions, and challenge. Again, the general education teacher has now been targeted to focus on low-performing students to the degree that little time is left for the creativity and stretching needed for the highest performing advanced learners. The problem is highlighted in some Advanced Placement (AP) courses where mixed-ability grouping is the trend. AP teachers often have to slow down the pace or spend additional time on remediation rather than acceleration, which may benefit some but harm the level of performance of others.

Again, I must clarify that I am not advocating for returning to learning tracks where students do not have the benefit of learning from the strengths of one another. Nor am I advocating for certain students to lose access to AP courses and curriculum. I am not advocating for segregated classes. We have already identified the errors of that pathway. I am not advocating that all students should not have access to high-level content teaching. As you will see, I am one of the strongest advocates for the contrary—all students should have the benefits of high-level content, teaching, learning, and functioning.

Although it is not popular to admit, there are some students that have a jump start ahead of the knowledge and abilities of others. There are going to be degrees of capabilities for people who have different abilities and different strengths as a fact of life. Some are going to be ahead, and it is true that we are all going to have to help those who are far behind. The realization is that some students (approximately 1–5 percent) have far more capabilities than others, and their needs cannot be met without specialized teacher development and advanced courses and content in the same way we have addressed struggling learners. Highly advanced learners need highly qualified teachers for their needs. The truth is, there are not a great number of teachers who are prepared to teach the most highly gifted and talented students. This is another area where teachers can benefit from additional development.

What I *am* suggesting is that RtI can assist in the appropriate identification and instruction of highly advanced students and their special needs as well. Using RtI framework, either the pyramid of interventions can be inverted, placing the most advanced students at the top of the pyramid at Tier 3 (representing the top 1–2 percent), or the students who have great potential for advanced work in the general population of students could be placed in the universal Tier 1 for support (representing the top 25 percent).

There are probably another 5–10 percent of the students who are what is considered as having "gifted potential." These students often are underdeveloped and underserved also. They function in heterogeneous groupings in general classrooms with specific support, but they need additional experiences in advanced and challenging ways. They should be placed in Tier 2 of the pyramid.

For this RtI adaptation, the universal Tier 1 model is preferred. An RtI framework that can be developed for gifted and talented learners might include the following:

- *Tier 1* (gifted/talented potential, highly proficient, and advanced learners who struggle): Universal assessments are administered in class to determine which students require interventions based on advanced skills development. Instruction in core curriculum with differentiated lessons for advanced learners in specific advanced groupings is required. Teaching and progress monitoring for deep-level understanding is needed. Students can work in mixed-ability groups, encouraging peer learning. Data is gathered by the general education teacher to determine if a referral is needed for placement in an advanced student pathway. Reliable alternative assessment tools are needed to identify students who have gifted education potential, especially students who appear "smart" and are English-language learners or are from low-income families or families of color. These students are often omitted from gifted education classes and programs due to the fact that their gifted areas are not identified and nurtured.

Tier 1 is intended for all students who are taught in the general classroom. Particular attention is paid to the top 25+ percent of students who perform above the proficient and at the advanced level who may need additional support. Selected students might be placed in AP courses other than the general classroom with guidance and strong, monitored support and assistance. Caution must be taken to ensure that gaps and omissions in advanced knowledge and thinking are noted and interventions are provided at various levels of intensity. Student interests and special talents should be explored in and out of school with academic and special interests mentors.

- *Tier 2* (gifted learners who struggle and advanced learners): Students should be evaluated through universal screening for above-grade-level mastery of core curriculum. Group and individual assessments are needed to define and determine individual mental and intellectual abilities, capabilities, aptitude, and appropriate grade-level acceleration placement in various areas for different populations of students. Included should be measures that consider language, culture, and socioeconomic factors. These students may require coteaching, clustering, or a pullout program taught by a gifted education specialist with progress monitoring. Tier 2 is intended for the top 10–15 percent of advanced students who score beyond peers and may need facilitation and support for continued development.

A "child find team" prepares a comprehensive learning plan, including interventions for students who need support to catch up with more advanced peers. Extensions of the core curriculum, supplemental, enrichment, independent, and extended study should be taught. Students can demonstrate understanding of core curriculum and concepts with flexibility. These students should participate in AP courses with support. Student interests and special talents should be explored and nurtured in and out of school through structured independent study, I Search projects, extension courses matched to special interests and abilities, and so forth. Mentors and specialized teachers or guides should be involved in the development of these students.

- *Tier 3* (highly gifted/talented learners): Through universal screening, these students have mastered core content and require various levels of complexity to delve deeper and apply questions, research, and understanding across disciplines. Students are evaluated for more-than-above-grade-level acceleration, gifted and talented program placement, and early college or other advanced classes and programs. Some students might be placed in Tier 3 for interventions based on capabilities and support in AP and dual-enrollment college courses or be supplied mentors, teacher coaches, and after-school programs. This would address the underrepresentation of disadvantaged learners in gifted education programs.

Tier 3 is intended for the top 2–5 percent of students who perform far beyond their peers, who may need specialized placement or programs several grades beyond the norm. These are learners who are flexible in their thinking, use knowledge in advanced ways, are mature in the performance and demonstration of knowledge, and are sophisticated in the level of understanding. Student interests and special talents should be explored in and out of school through specialized mentors, coaches, programs, community or university experiences, internships, independent study/research/inquiry, and so on.

Some gifted and talented students are nontraditional learners or have been diagnosed as "twice exceptional," meaning that they have a learning disability in addition to giftedness. RtI models should be explored and expanded to provide ILPs for these students as well. Our nation will not reach its potential if the specific educational needs of some students are sacrificed for the benefit of others.

Somehow we must lift all students to meet America's promise. Of special note is a group of students who sometimes are among the most unidentified gifted and talented students in our classrooms. They are often disengaged youth, who as a group account for the disproportionate amount of school failure. They have the highest school dropout rate, the least degree of academic achievement, and the lowest test scores as compared to all of their peers, male and female. We are talking about the school performance data that has been generated over time relative to African American males.

Unfortunately, many African American boys have to dance a fine line between academic and ethnic identity. As Jonathan Livingston and Cinawendela Nahimana (2006) put it, is it a "problem child or problem context"? Although we seek equitable learning, the reality is that we educate different children differently. Most school effects studies document that, among other barriers, many black males suffer from a lack of a sense of belonging in school, lack of educational aspirations, lack of academic self-efficacy, and negative feedback, treatment, and school and curriculum practices. In order to capture the "gifted-ness" of these students, prevention and intervention processes are needed to provide a "bridge" as African American gifted males attempt to navigate a perilous social, economic, and educational environment.

CHAPTER 5

The Black Male Agenda

The old arrow is a model for the craftsman making a new one.

African proverb

AN OUT-OF-SCHOOL SNAPSHOT: THE BRIDGE

Learning gaps, performance gaps, achievement gaps, college matriculation gaps, economic gaps, gender gaps, racial gaps, family gaps, experience gaps—these all apply to the dilemmas of black males' life in our nation, and in fact in many parts of the world. Disproportionate rates of school failure, school dropouts, referrals for special education services, and incarceration all speak to a need for focused interventions that counteract structural and environmental impacts on many black families and children, especially black males. Like a Ferris wheel that goes around and around, sometimes the search for solutions can be found in past efforts.

Troubling to many in America is the exclusion of black boys and men from economic, social, educational, and political life. Changes in society's traditions and ill-fated schooling have resulted in higher attendance problems, lower high school and college completion rates, and high levels of crime by disenfranchised people in communities, especially African Americans. Some of the problem is attributed to subtleties in differences between boys and girls—how males in general learn and are motivated, and how they are expected to conform to a women-dominated teaching force. Sax (2007) raised the concern that there is widespread disengagement of boys in school and in life that is affecting every racial and socioeconomic group of males.

Sax cites the fact that smaller proportions of males are going to colleges, and changes in the educational formula and curricula over the past twenty to thirty years have contributed to undermotivation and underachievement of men. He suggested that the performance of males has been negatively affected by the acceleration of early learning curriculum, a shift to an academic intellectual orientation, a move away from active learning such as hands-on, a move away from competition and athletics, and fewer vocational/technical offerings, structured physical education programs, and experiential learning including field trips.

If these viewpoints are accurate, then the plight of black males is twofold. It might serve us well to evaluate how theory and practice of education over the past thirty to forty years, with its changes, have disengaged a large proportion of boys from school, especially black boys. We have discussed one high school intervention, the AdvancePath academies in chapter 4, that has turned out to be successful for both high school males and females, with impressive impact on Latino and black males. Additional interventions are needed both inside and outside the education system to more aggressively support black and Latino male students, and others as well.

Many out-of-school initiatives are being implemented to strengthen the capacity to improve the outcomes for teens in the areas of education, work, and life. Certainly not all black males suffer from these disparities, nor are all at risk. Many value the purpose of schooling and look forward to upward mobility that successful schooling can bring. As result, many black males have progressed through public school, advancing to college completion and successful careers and families. However, associated with those accomplishments comes cultural values placed on maintaining a "black man's" identity, which is an integral component of their achievements and self-identity. This is a fine dance for black males that involves being able to resolve the tug-of-war between academic excellence and street survival.

For many black males, especially teens in the United States, the profile of success noted above is not applicable. The reality is that far too many are knee-deep in educational, social, economic, unemployment, life, and family obstacles, requiring serious prevention and intervention measures. Having observed successful prevention and intervention programs and strategies for these youths, the myth can be dispelled that black males are generally "anti-intellectual" and uninterested in pursuing academic goals. If given the appropriate school culture and learning environment, and the right motivation and context, many who are traditionally considered at risk will aspire to go beyond high school completion to achieve responsibility, pride, and success in life.

Often these students require a structure and system support organized around their needs and cultural dispositions. If provided cultural and youth understandings and a trusting and supportive academic and social environment, many black teens and youths who are perceived as disengaged will work feverishly to complete their education and earn a diploma. If given a viable chance to succeed with the right adults, they diligently rise to the occasion. Some of these black males are the brightest, most intelligent students, who simply do not succeed in the traditional construct of public schooling. Because these students are heavily influenced by out-of-school inclinations, help and support are needed from the community and society at large.

Two African American males, Ed Woodley and Kevin Curvey-Preston, who at the time were involved in an at-risk program for teens that focused on personal, academic, and vocational/technical development and support, contributed excerpts to an article published in *Curriculum Context*, the journal of the Washington State Association for Supervision and Curriculum Development, in 1991. Kevin was a teaching assistant in the Department of Elementary and Secondary Education at Washington State University and was working on his master's in education. The stories that he shared about the challenges and successes of the youth involved in the program were intriguing.

Kevin and Edwin were encouraged to join me in documenting their work. That led to a publication about the complexities and issues black males face and the potential for finding ways to put the building blocks in place to support student learning and life success. In 1991, Edwin joined Medina Children's Service, an organization that placed children in private homes in Seattle. The BRIDGE Program grew out of the need to address male and female issues of personal and family responsibilities.

This was one of the first comprehensive interventions designed to meet the needs of two targeted populations: youths age thirteen to sixteen and seventeen- to twenty-five-year-olds. Many of the overall goals of existing parenting programs as well as current-day RtI components were incorporated. Prevention of teen pregnancies was emphasized, while at the same time issues that young men and women face as potential or actual teen parents were addressed.

As you will see, youth problems have not changed, with the exception that today the list has expanded to include school violence; bullying (including cyberbullying); date rape; abuse by trusted adults such as teachers, coaches, religious leaders, and family members; gay bashing; and HIV/AIDS and other sexually transmitted diseases, to name a few.

The breakdown of the nuclear family structure, increased exposure to technology and explicit media, changing societal norms and mores, and risky behaviors are a few of the shifts that have led to greater intensities of negative influences that affect youth. Let's rewind to one such program that served youth from K–12 education to community.

EXPANDING THE AGENDA: BUILDING A
NEW SYSTEM OF OPPORTUNITY FOR YOUTH

Searetha Smith, Kevin Curvey-Preston, and F. Edwin Woodley

[The following is reprinted by permission from *Curriculum in Context* 21 (1991), no. 2, 26–29.]

Youths-at-risk programs have evolved. However, oftentimes they result in incomplete strategies that do not address issues of student success or failure rates. . . . Historically, American society supported the idea of parent/student and teacher/student relationships as a means of educating [students]. Included in this traditional approach [was] the notion that parents should create support for education in the home. Presently these notions appear passé. Changes in conditions today [include] single parenting, [the necessity] for dual income families, working parents, [no parents], students parenting themselves, etc. The support base that schools enjoyed in the past have changed. . . . Parenting roles [have changed], but the educational process and expectations remain the same.

This has created a communication breakdown, sometimes making contact, support, and collaborative involvement difficult or nonexistent among students, teachers, and parents. . . . Some students do not have the educational or social skills to survive in a traditional system because no one has taught those skills to them. As a result, a segment of society has developed that consists of people who are unprepared to succeed and participate in school or the future society.

In many school settings, at-risk youths are not developing the skills to function in the education system. . . . "To be effective, school programs must be constructed around the interest and experiences of at-risk youth" (Forys, 1989). [Also] suggested [was] the need to have program solutions that focus on a more coherent strategy for reclaiming and redirecting youths who are at risk of failure. [Forys] outlined four different and sometimes overlapping considerations for developing intervention/prevention programs:

1. Personal problems such as substance abuse, juvenile delinquency, or homelessness;
2. Teenage pregnancy and parenthood;
3. Poor school performance and dissatisfaction with the school environment; and
4. Economic hardships.

The Response

BRIDGE: A New System of Opportunity . . . specifically addressed young men and women who came from highly dysfunctional families. These students stopped attending school and became years behind in credits. Most had encounters with courts and social service systems. Some deal drugs, most abuse alcohol. Some carry guns and are involved in gangs.

Few hold jobs or have prospects for employment beyond the lowest-level positions. Most significantly, many of these young men are fathering babies or engaging in unprotected sex. Some have girlfriends. Others experience casual encounters. While many are proud of fathering children, few have the financial, social, or emotional resources needed to deal with the practical and legal obligations of parenthood.

BRIDGE was developed to redefine and implement an effective program focusing on personal, academic, and vocational needs of at-risk youths. The BRIDGE system grew out of a program funded by the U.S. Office of Health. It was intended for young men and women who are at-risk of not receiving a successful socialization experience in their family or educational situations. [Therefore], the program had implications for school districts, university training programs, and [stakeholders who directly or] indirectly were responsible for integrating various services for youth.

Mr. Woodley and Curvey-Preston assessed myriad obstacles challenging youth—the economic need, single-parent homes, racial prejudice, school failure, parenthood, drugs, and the temptation to steal. Working with facilitators from the community, the BRIDGE curriculum and case management system was developed. The program provided tangible benefits such as job placement, job-hunting tips, parenting education, and health information. More important, it included exercising classes, one-to-one counseling and group sessions that focus on intangibles such as self-esteem, responsibility, alternatives to anger, and resisting street pressure.

Having worked with at-risk youths, Mr. Woodley discovered that the key issue for many young men and women is child support. Entry-level jobs that could be obtained paid little, and some young men had as much as $400 a month for child support garnished from their wages by the courts. Since they have little vocational training in public schools, few have marketable skills for career employment. Thus, the present system encourages reliance on illegal activities to supplement their incomes.

The Path Across the BRIDGE

Youths were referred for participation in the BRIDGE system from a wide variety of community agencies and BRIDGE outreach workers. Working with case managers, each participant developed a plan to complete their education, begin work training, and acquire the socialization skills [required] in the educational system and workplace. Case managers were responsible for guiding participants through the BRIDGE system. They received bonuses when participants finished the program and completed six months [in job placement].

Teens were matched to a volunteer mentor [who taught and tutored] the skills necessary [for survival in the workplace]. Mentors introduced participants to a positive cultural learning environment, and [helped with] basic communication skills that nurtured transition into the workplace and learning setting. After successful completion of this training, participants were eligible for paid internships, working at the BRIDGE industrial facility, under expert supervision of employees or volunteers provided by local industry.

Participants who completed the BRIDGE internship were matched to job opportunities, and the case managers conducted follow-up. At the time of job placement, participants who had children on public assistance met with the case manager and [a representative] from the Office of Support Enforcement to modify and update the youth's child-support plan.

Evaluation

The project director and the staff met monthly to track the progress of activities and ensure that target dates were met. A coalition composed of juvenile corrections, mental health, public health, judiciary officials, representatives from the business and private sector, volunteers from community support groups, educational institutions, and families met quarterly to assess the program. The coalition ensured that the project was executed in accordance with local and federal guidelines.

With this design, the hope was that the BRIDGE system would quantify the effects that volunteer and mentor case management and group sessions had on youth. [Also,] they sought [to find out the] effects that increased employment potential had on reducing criminal involvement and maintaining employment. The system was structured to prevent "program addiction," which implied a dependent rather than an independent effect. Staff was motivated and rewarded at each stage to ensure that youth successfully completed the program and [were prepared to participate] in the community as parents and employees without dependence on the BRIDGE system.

At the heart of the BRIDGE system was intervention and prevention, but also provision of practical, tangible benefits. These students needed a way to earn money while pursuing their education, career, and work aspirations. To that end, the BRIDGE Program developed academic and vocational skills, and provided individual and group counseling that focused on tangibles and intangibles essential to self, community, and family responsibility.

A suggested vision for the BRIDGE program included adding a component to provide an educational path leading to obtaining a high school diploma as opposed to a General Education Development (GED). Efforts were planned to collaborate and work on transition and entry into a two-year or four-year school of higher education. These changes were intended to help students realize more economic and career opportunities and benefits over their lifetime. Future strategies that were considered were:

1. Link with specific local school districts and colleges of higher education;
2. Build support systems in schools of higher education and the workplace; and
3. Place students in academic, applied academic, and/or vocational education or technical schools.

The BRIDGE system gave students the help needed to build improved systems for lifelong learning and success. It provided help for students to perform in acceptable ways (Smith, 1990). Only by developing [academic], career/technical and vocational skills, and caring capacities can conditions for youth completely improve. Commitment and effort to educate without collaboration or shared resources are useless.

Educators are not trained to be social or health service providers, law enforcers, public officials, family workers, drug enforcers, or counselors. Although some teacher-training programs attempt to develop skills in these areas, teachers do not have the time or expertise to devote the appropriate amount of effort to providing these services. . . . If schools continue to function as the providers of myriad social, health, [societal, family,] and educational needs of students, they will continue to fail a large number of their students. . . . Coalitions [must be developed] to help eliminate barriers and build bridges to success. It is only through this process that all students have the opportunity to learn and succeed [reprinted material ends].

IMPLICATIONS FOR TODAY

The BRIDGE Program offered insight into how to intervene in attitudes and behaviors of teens and youths who struggle with adversity and overwhelming obstacles and who suffer from social injustices. Sometimes these youngsters display "tough" exteriors and seem aloof and disinterested. Often this is a facade to deliver the message that they are in control and can navigate their environment in the cultural context in which they interact and live.

While this chapter has focused on the plight of black males, it must be noted that the concerns and discussion apply to other males and females who have similar issues. Many of the same behaviors and needs can also be seen in Latino and Native American males and their plight. In addition, the BRIDGE Program has implications for how school districts can form advocacy and partnerships to share the roles and responsibilities for assisting students who are challenged.

Elements of Response to Intervention protocols and procedures could be shared with out-of-school agencies and sources to lessen the load on schools and teachers. Schools could focus more attention on academic development and college, career, and workplace readiness and proficiencies. Out-of-school providers and agencies would then serve the role of focusing and assisting with nonacademic supports and competencies.

Although the BRIDGE Program was implemented some time ago, its features and intent are relevant to RtI, student learning, and youth life today. Unfortunately, the BRIDGE Program lost its funding and is no longer in existence. This has implications for federal and state policies, funding, and support for sustaining prevention and intervention programs that prove effective. Why reinvent the wheel when promising and evidence-based models have already been demonstrated? Schools and outside agencies could pool resources to re-create and preserve interventions that are geared to different populations of teens and young adults. Safety nets would seamlessly be in place for the plethora of problems and challenges of teens and youths.

SOCIETY   WORLD

High Risk Students

Socialization

Clinical Support
Social Agencies

Pre-K-12 Education

Diploma

Technical Training
with Workplace
Mentors

Post Secondary
Education

Our Goal!

A Good Citizen
Role Model in
the Community

**MERGING AT RISK YOUNG MEN
AND WOMEN, INTO A DRUG AND
CRIME FREE ORIENTATION
THROUGH EDUCATION, POST -
SECONDARY AND WORKPLACE
SKILLS TRAINING, CLINICAL
SUPPORT AND SOCIALIZATION**

Career & Work
Experience

Acceptance
of Family
Responsibilities

Career/Job Placement

Vocational/Technical
Workplace Placement

Permission by Curriculum Context. Adapted by Searetha Smith-Collins (2011). From: Smith, Preston-Curvey. & Woodley (1993). Expanding the agenda. Building a new system of opportunity for youths (1993). Curriculum in Context. Journal of Washington State Association of Supervision and Curriculum, Washington. 21(2). 26-29.

Figure 5.1. *A Bridge of Opportunity for At-Risk Youth*

CHAPTER 6

Assessing the Outcomes

All change is not growth, as all movement is not forward.

Ellen Glasgow (in Lewis, Garrison-Wade,
Scott, Douglass, & Middleton [2004])

Before the outcomes of Response to Intervention can be assessed, consensus must be built around the essential belief systems that underlie philosophical and operation principles. Areas to grapple with for decades to come will include the following:

1. Overcoming racial, gender, and socioeconomic barriers to equal access and examining the instructional program as it relates to equitable, measurable learning school-wide.
2. Personalizing the learning process for each student and teacher. Just as with students, some teachers have stronger skills and ability levels than others.
3. In this period of change, the desperate need for retraining of teachers and school leaders who can meet the demands of today's schools will continue to be urgent.
4. Teachers must receive more support, including how to teach the structure of language and reading skills and how to apply those skills at all levels.
5. For mathematics, breaking down abstract concepts and number sense in relevant, concrete ways to provide solid foundations and understanding, starting in kindergarten through grade 12, is needed.
6. A common understanding of the expectations and complexities of education requires attention. If not, challenges and expectations will remain undefined and frustrating for principals and teachers.
7. Teachers must receive time, opportunity, experience, and support to acquire the complex skills, attributes, intuition, ideals, and preparation needed to become masterful. Burns and Ysseldyke (2006) estimate that

it takes a period of four to almost ten years for a teacher to develop that level of expertise.

Inherent in the assessment agenda, tools are needed to measure progress toward the above ideals. The persistent problem of defining appropriate criteria for qualitative indicators such as confidence and instinct is not replicable or scalable. Also, it is important to know how different intervention models affect student outcomes. Several concerns need to be acknowledged when reviewing the effectiveness of RtI models:

1. Research has been conducted on a limited number of implementations.
2. There is a lack of measurement on the longevity of effectiveness of models.
3. Early studies use different definitions and measures of effectiveness.
4. Correlation studies are needed to distinguish other factors that might have contributed to success.
5. Follow-up and further study is needed to determine if findings can be generalized and replicated in other contexts.

NATIONAL OUTCOMES (ACADEMIC)

The good news is that early findings appear promising. Following are some of the outcomes that have been reported in various parts of the country.

- Long Beach, California: Seventy-three percent of more than 150 schools are meeting California state standards. African American and Hispanic students outpaced white students on gains on the STAR (California state assessment, which includes the Stanford 9 Standardized Achievement Test).
- Knox County, Tennessee (which includes the Knoxville Public Schools): The number of students with disabilities identified was reduced from 22.3 percent of the student population (11,596) to 13.2 percent (6,996).
- The Minneapolis Public Schools reduced the achievement gap for African American students. African Americans responded more quickly than any other ethnic group of students to strategic (Tier 2) interventions. Disproportionate numbers of African Americans placed in special education decreased over a three-year period (Billingsly, 2009).
- Vail Unified School District outside of Tucson, Arizona: VanDerHeyden, Witt, and Gilbertson (2007) reported on a multiyear, staggered study of the implementation of a systemic RtI model. The focus was on the identification of students for special education services across five elementary schools. The System to Enhance Educational Performance (STEEP) model was implemented for class-wide universal screening of reading

and mathematics skills. Individual interventions decreased the numbers of student referrals for special education services, and overidentification of students of color and males was reduced (Sparks, 2011; VanDerHeyden, Witt, & Gilbertson, 2007).

NATIONAL OUTCOMES (BEHAVIORAL)

- The Los Angeles Unified School District reported that, among a group of Latino immigrants with clinical and depressive Posttraumatic Stress Disorder (PTSD), an intervention program using the Cognitive Behavioral Intervention for Trauma in Schools (CBITS) demonstrated statistically significant reductions in PTSD and depressive symptoms as compared to the control group students. The intervention is being used with the general population of students in the school district. Also, it has been effectively implemented with a wide range of racially and ethnically diverse children. Adaptations are being developed for Native American children, non-English speakers, and recent immigrants who speak primary languages such as Spanish, Russian, Korean, and Western Armenian (Los Angeles Unified School District, 2011).
- In Illinois and Hawaii over a three-year period, schools implementing School-Wide Positive Behavior Supports (SWPBS) had 25 percent fewer office disciplinary referrals than a comparison group of schools not implementing similar supports. Although the need for future research was indicated, training and technical assistance were functionally related to improved implementation of universal SWPBS practices. Improvements in the perceived safety of the school setting and the proportion of third graders meeting or exceeding state reading assessment standards were noted (Homer, Sugai, Smolkowski, Eber, Nakasoto, Todd, & Esperanza, 2009).
- A school in Illinois reported an 85 percent decrease in suspensions following two years of RtI implementation. This same school reported the proportion of students meeting or exceeding proficiency on the Illinois State Achievement Test (ISAT) increased by 14 percentage points in reading and 24 in math (Billingsly, 2009).

MEASURING SUCCESS

Measures and definitions of success continue to be complicated. For example, there is no clarity on how to apply RtI effectively or apply the process for specific purposes. More specifically, there is no consensus as to whether RtI should become a part of the identification process for students with disabilities or on the effectiveness of movement between levels of intensity of interventions.

Finally, there are concerns that RtI is spreading ahead of its research base. Educators may not know with certainty which component is the "egg" (cause) and which is the "chicken" (effect). The current research focus is on isolated pieces, such as the effects of interventions at various tiers, data analysis and decision-making, and teacher training. Few studies have been made on the entire RtI model—separating the dynamics of evidence-based reading instruction from the RtI process, for instance.

Although there are mounting questions, RtI appears promising for addressing special-needs students and others with limited abilities for success in school.

CHAPTER 7

The Learning Target

Learning is not attained by chance, it must be sought with ardor and attended to with diligence.

Abigail Adams, 1780

TEACH, TEST, AND HOPE FOR THE BEST

Let's refer back to two earlier questions: How can teachers make Response to Intervention work in the regular classroom, and how can teachers truly provide strength-based teaching for every child? All teachers and leaders must be clear on the academic goals of the system. Then they can make goals work with conviction for all students. This step is the most basic requirement for RtI implementation. The appropriateness of the curriculum and the importance of students receiving the intended curriculum taught by a qualified teacher are the first criteria for understanding why students might have learning difficulties. In other words, the *curriculum matters*.

The reasonableness of how everything ties together must be considered. It all begins with a preK–12 articulated curriculum that is designed to accommodate all learners. Teachers have the awesome responsibility of managing curriculum and instruction, including core, elective, enrichment, advanced, special-needs, supplemental, modified, and adjusted education. In addition, they must focus on the expected accompanying teaching and learning strategies, mandated learning standards, materials, and assessments. This all has to be done according to achievement data, best practices, and state, federal, local, district, and school requirements.

In doing all of this, one has to figure out how to weave the critical pieces into a whole by managing and organizing the learning environment and the various student requirements, and maintaining on-task behavior (even for students who have few abilities to manage themselves). When determining decisions about curriculum, the teacher must consider the following:

- What should I be teaching?
- What strategies and materials should I use?
- How should I assess student learning?
- Who has mastery of the essential objectives?
- Upon analysis and reflection, what adjustments are needed?

All of this is done with student outcomes and teacher evaluation in mind.

From the viewpoint of the learner, systemic, articulated curriculum goals and objectives are essential to coherent teaching and learning. If any component of the curriculum and instruction process is not mastered, breakdowns in learning can occur. Before considering RtI and all of its promise, we must take a step back and evaluate the strength of the curriculum in general education as the foundation.

In many large urban school districts that are targets of the national reform, all curriculum expectations come to a halt during the months of March, April, and May, the "testing season." There is a period in many public schools when "teaching to the test" becomes the priority. This is a time when many schools, especially low-performing ones, drop everything, including teaching the intended curriculum and course syllabi, to develop test-taking skills and prepare for high-stakes standardized tests. Usually this occurs when there is a punitive threat associated with school closure, school takeover, teacher and staff firings, or entire school reconstitution associated with school reform sanctions for not meeting annual yearly progress targets. The hope is to show significant improvement in student outcomes by focusing on simulated practice tests, test-taking skills, and parallel content.

Improved test scores are of high significance to teachers and principals because they are linked to jobs and livelihoods. For a desperate few, this has allegedly meant going to such extreme measures as prompting students on the high-stakes tests during administration. Some teachers and leaders have been disciplined for changing student answers to ensure that accountability targets are met. Of course, these behaviors are not acceptable or indicative of the ethics and professional behavior of most educators.

Although this behavior is not excusable, it is not surprising to think a human response to a negative, untenable high-stakes environment could cause some humans to go to desperate measures. This situation wreaks havoc on general classroom pedagogy (the ways teachers orchestrate classroom learning).

Rather than teach the depth and breadth of essential knowledge for under-standing, meaning, and transferability, the standardized test has become front and center with the hope that students will do their best.

Those who oppose the "teach, test, and hope for the best" syndrome are calling for a commonsense emphasis on teaching subject matter efficiently, effectively, and more deeply over time. Their strategy is to help students learn so they can synthesize information in ways that are integrated and applied to various situations, including on high-stakes national tests.

All of this comes at a time when educators should be focusing on whether or not the general curriculum is manageable, clear, coherent, and effectively taught to all students. The focus has to be returned to six key areas of appro-priateness for teaching and learning:

1. Learning standards
2. Curriculum and teaching for understanding
3. Instruction and student support systems
4. Equitable treatment and opportunity
5. Availability of appropriate materials and resources, including technol-ogy and digital tools
6. Quality of the available staff and ongoing development and training to support teachers and other staff

MOVING FROM RANDOM ACTS OF CURRICULUM AND INSTRUCTION

Constancy of purpose should be directed at effective delivery of the expected curriculum. Then isolated parts or various educational transformational efforts can be assessed on their individual or collective merits in relation to curricu-lum expectations. RtI and other desired instructional strategies could operate in harmony with identified district and curriculum goals.

Acquiring deep-level knowledge and rigor requires paying attention to the sequence of a systemic curriculum design. Then the task is to match the cur-riculum to instructional strategies, resources, and assessment. Ruth Herman Wells, in her article "Is It Time to Swap K-12 Education Trends for Common Sense Solutions?" (2011), states:

> With no curriculum in place to ensure that School Skills are taught, it should be no surprise that so many students have difficulty arriving on time, focusing, participating and doing the work that's expected. Until you teach youngsters ad-dition and subtraction, they'll never master long division. Until we systematically

and comprehensively teach School Skills—attendance, punctuality, motivation, how to participate in class discussions, respect for teachers, homework management, and how to focus—many youngsters will never master being students. Even though many teachers take it upon themselves to remedy gaps in children's training to be students, those efforts can't compensate for what is essentially a random, non-system of non-instruction. The child can't swim because no one has taught the child to be a swimmer. The child can't succeed in school because no one has taught the child to be a student.

Educational experiences for students with disabilities are shared between general and special education teachers. In a U.S. Department of Education survey conducted in 2000, only 32 percent of public school teachers who taught students with disabilities indicated they were well prepared to address the needs of these students (Parsad, Lewis, & Ferris, 2001). Special and general education teachers and related service providers (speech and language therapists, occupational therapists, social workers, etc.) usually are not connected directly to a systemic approach to curriculum and professional development.

Everything should be aligned to improve the management, coordination, and implementation of the intended core curriculum. After a reliable curriculum is in place, teachers can provide initial and ongoing instruction to strengthen and improve content knowledge to meet expected learning goals. Collaborative professional development should help general and special education teachers and others demonstrate more significant content knowledge and skills in targeted areas.

A solid curriculum plan becomes a meaningful way for teachers to approach relationships among learning, activities, and results. It becomes the basis for joint efforts and reflections about the ability to achieve improvements. A coherent preK–12 curriculum should be taught to "regular" students, then made applicable to others, including highly capable students. This is the starting point for individual school improvement planning.

COMMON LANGUAGE, COMMON MISSION

Before proceeding further, let's clarify terms for the purpose of developing common language and understanding—the first step in any curriculum design process. *Curriculum* refers to organized sets of experiences that are meaningfully connected. Curriculum can be organized into manageable modules, units, chunks, or lessons. It can include organized sets of purposeful experiences in school, the home, and the community. Curriculum experiences help students develop their potential for learning.

Instruction, in contrast to curriculum, is the way or system used to deliver organized sets of experiences. Curriculum drives instruction, not vice versa. Instruction utilizes instructional materials, interventions, and supplemental materials or programs, which are not curricula. Teachers develop instructional goals, objectives, and lessons as opposed to textbook chapters, programmed materials, or software as substitutes for curriculum.

Students should show mastery of content at different levels of complexity based on common learning standards (research-based content that identifies key areas of curriculum). Accommodations or modifications to the curriculum and learning standards are required for students with learning differences and disabilities.

Extending the definition of curriculum to the home and community has important implications for school success. Although students spend time in school, it may not necessarily be the place where the greater time is spent on learning. The home and community can be a more significant influence on learning than school. Even though many school districts extend the day and school year, implement before- and after-school programs, hold Saturday school, and so forth, the actual in-school learning time is greatly consumed by nonacademic endeavors.

For some students more than others, significant amounts of out-of-school time are spent home alone, in child care or recreation centers, with peers, on street corners, watching unsupervised television, console or online gaming, on Facebook and other social media sites updating, texting, tweeting, and so on. The time spent may be more or less, but the implication is that students spend a significant amount of time learning in other settings outside school.

It is important to say that home and community matter, and therefore they cannot be omitted from the formula for improvement. Out-of-school curriculum can either enhance or complicate school learning and behavior. Unity of purpose and coordination of effort for school readiness and student achievement can be woven into the plan to optimize learning experiences.

Using this as philosophical background information, the following is an aggregate case history of an academic curriculum leader's efforts to design systemic curriculum and instructional coordination across grade and school levels. The major goals were to:

1. help teachers reflect on their practice;
2. provide criteria upon which to base activities, dialogue, instruction, and intervention decisions;
3. optimize instruction prior to the need for intervention; and

4. generate questions, clarify goals, and ensure curriculum continuity for the learner.

OPTIMIZING CURRICULUM FOR ALL: THE LEARNING TARGET

Improving instruction and achievement was the key issue that inspired Everybody's School District in Anywhere, America, to piece together a process of curriculum redesign. Helping students successfully use and integrate information served as the catalyst. Over a period of three years, this school district of more than 20,500 students worked at the forefront of designing a unified curriculum framework that would optimize learning for all students. Improvement efforts were guided by eliminating three major curriculum issues that are known to create inconsistent, disconnected curriculum goals, outcomes, and opportunities for students:

1. Fragmentation/segmentation
2. Redundancy/repetition
3. Gaps and omission

In addition, the aim was to develop a common vision through:

- designing a focused preK–12, goal-centered, meaningful curriculum that eliminated duplication and fractured delivery;
- prioritizing and identifying essential core skills, content, and performance standards and expected outcomes;
- providing a guiding framework for curriculum, instruction, and assessment; and
- creating the synergy to put together various pieces of content and pedagogy to teach varied students at a high level.

The district's conservative reputation did not support the willingness to change. Levels of cooperation for achieving consensus and improving curriculum were lacking. Teachers, principals, staff, parents, and students were enlisted to add qualitative data (comments, observations, concerns, artifacts, etc.) for more insight into the district's quantitative data (standardized test data on student learning, graduation, attendance, dropout data, etc.). Consistent data indicated a systematic preK–12 curriculum that could be differentiated for all learners was needed.

Two years of graduate follow-up studies confirmed the finding. Approximately half of 2,376 graduates agreed that high school experiences in the district encouraged learning and generally were pleasant and rewarding occurrences. Student comments echoed consistent themes:

1. Classes could have been more challenging.
2. Students could have better prepared for higher education.
3. Courses could have been more relevant to work and real-life situations.

This information served as further validation of the need to redesign and improve the curriculum to fit requirements for raising the bar for more highly knowledgeable, technically prepared graduates who could transition into the global society. Parents, students, and community members were generally supportive of the district; however, some felt their voices had been ignored in the past. They had already expressed the need to upgrade curriculum and instructional approaches.

It was important to acknowledge that the school district had some of the highest test scores in the area. In general, they were substantially higher than state and national averages. Consistent with many affluent school districts, teacher assessments indicated the majority of district students met expectations. However, they concurred that there was a need for higher-level course requirements. Even though the district excelled on standardized tests, there were specific schools and pockets of students that did not flourish. The target expanded to convincing people that there was the need for making a good school district even better.

The leader cautiously began to work with staff to examine three major questions:

1. How did the curriculum help all students have the access and opportunity to meet the expected learning standards?
2. How could restructuring change the curriculum so that it was appropriate for any student regardless of ability or special needs?
3. How could curriculum restructuring result in systemic change that would provide opportunities for all students to access essential learning?

The approach was first to design a solid general education curriculum that could be modified and differentiated for differently abled students, including the highly capable. A second goal was then to embed key components that would allow students to receive instructional opportunities to reach established learning standards. Teachers need a coherent curriculum, instructional strategies, resources, and predicable intervention techniques to help all students reach their full potential.

The academic leader was aware that the teachers needed time to learn and assimilate curriculum development, instructional strategies, resources, interventions, and training. Being a new academic leader in a conservative school district where change was not readily embraced, it was necessary to be mindful not to "throw the baby out with the bathwater." The majority of the staff did not feel there was a need to change their individual or school curriculum.

Very reluctantly, hundreds of staff members were brought together to develop preK–12 curriculum frameworks for seven disciplines: social studies, physical education, science, health, English/language arts, fine arts, and mathematics. Overarching themes for each discipline expressed the "why"—the "big ideas" or purposes for teaching. For example, physical education focused on a theme of "Healthy Living Choices through Knowledge and Application." Health expanded the concept and integrated the theme "Wellness: Developing Mental, Physical, Social, and Emotional Balance through Responsible Choices."

Science utilized the overarching theme "Discovering and Exploring Patterns, Systems, and Cycles," which easily integrated with the mathematics department's "Patterns and Relationships: Investigating, Generalizing, Applying, and Communicating." Social studies focused on "Change, Participation, Diversity, and Interdependence throughout Systems," which adapted well to the theme for English/language arts: "Understanding Patterns, Identity, and Community: The Art of Communication." The theme was easily integrated for the fine arts department, which selected "A Universal Means of Communication through Creating, Performing, and Appreciating." The themes seemed to develop the synergy, clarity for their destination, and excitement needed to inspire defining how they were to get to the destination—the curriculum.

Fitting the Pieces Together

K–12 teachers sought opportunities for conversation about what curriculum is essential for students to understand at various levels. Other discussions of interest centered on what content was essential for teaching and learning and what it means to think conceptually and learn a discipline. Curriculum frameworks are based on the belief that it is critical to create a community of learners to struggle with the challenges of teaching high-quality content. In addition to the critical conversations, teachers must examine currently held beliefs.

Teachers must support the need to construct a more powerful way of developing curriculum understandings. They need time to reflect on their own learning and explore new beliefs and behaviors. A curriculum framework development process can foster a sense of community. It can serve as the vehicle for examining beliefs about teaching and learning. A curriculum design process can provide time needed for investigating instruction and intervention strategies and materials that promote stronger student learning.

With all of that in mind, communication about what curriculum was taught and how it was taught across grade levels became the impetus for understanding the need for coherence. Teachers determined which initiatives should be site based and which needed to have standards across the district. They debated opposing philosophies within and across disciplines and throughout school levels. Most important, they discussed the effects of the absence of a systemic approach to educating students.

Curriculum frameworks safeguard against attaching lessons and activities that facilitate the wrong intent. The design of the framework was approached as a new paradigm that would force people to move from past practices and ideas that had not proven effective. For example, teachers soon realized that the disconnection and fragmentation that occurred between grade and school levels was a critical inhibiting factor to student understanding.

Professional dialogue continued around expectations of the need to gauge student performance against existing and emerging international and national learning standards. Local guidance came from the district's strategic plan, which specified development of a comprehensive curriculum for all disciplines, matched to proposed common core standards. Often the debates centered on new school reform requirements and efforts, and there were controversial discussions about common core standards and assessments. Other lively conversations centered on rigorous course requirements and challenges in the field about various curriculum directions and philosophies. Curriculum restructuring felt more like jigsaw puzzle pieces that first had to be located before the puzzle could be put together.

The Design Process

After reviewing the literature, curricular practices revealed consistent issues of segmentation and lack of a comprehensive preK–12 curriculum for general or gifted education. In designing the process, it was important to involve all school levels in order to create a sense of empowerment for teachers. It was critical to maintain the integrity of school-based curriculum decisions and to balance the need for systemic learning experiences. A clear goal from the viewpoint of the curriculum staff was to develop a local curriculum rather than utilizing a framework from an outside source. This was a good decision, because the process was ahead of its time. Until recently, most curricula have been segmented into elementary and secondary models.

As a reflective side note, the challenge before the curriculum writers today is to design or identify a tool that offers varied student opportunities to participate in a rich curriculum. Restructuring the curriculum has progressed with the standards movement. There are many great curriculum models available throughout the country, and therefore it is a waste of time and resources to start with a clean slate. It is much easier to locate a satisfactory design, identify the missing or desired components, and adapt a best-practice design for local needs.

Getting back to the story, to gain support for curriculum restructuring, the following targets were established:

* Provide leadership training for curriculum supervisors and coordinators.
* Provide information to the executive leadership and cabinet members.
* Inform the school board of the need for a comprehensive curriculum and what was involved to reach that outcome.
* Research various models and invest in self-directed leadership activities to determine state-of-the-art curriculum designs.
* Collaborate with curriculum directors and those in and out of education who are recognized as experts to determine options for development.
* Develop a rationale for a curriculum preK–12 scope.
* Identify a process for curriculum design.

Various curriculum models were available, but most offerings did not identify how various learners could access the general curriculum. For instance, there was no understanding of how the curriculum could be accessed for gifted or alternative education, career/technical education, or English-language learner (ELL) students.

The academic/curriculum leader studied the design of gifted education curriculum models with the assistance of an expert from a national gifted education leadership organization. Together they were able to address development of highly capable learners, applying the process to general education. Through that approach, all students would be provided a curriculum with high-level content and skills development as an integral component. The design also offered opportunities to incorporate multicultural concepts, multiple intelligence theories, interdisciplinary learning, technology, interventions, and higher-order thinking as integral components rather than as curricular "add-ons."

To facilitate the change process, it was necessary to consider the readiness, preparation, and involvement levels of the staff. Curriculum in the district had been autonomous, determined by classroom teachers and individual schools; some teachers had depended on the sequence of chapters in textbooks. An action plan was developed with the following planning considerations:

- Budget, talent, energy level, and receptiveness of staff
- Time for conceptualizing the process
- Perspectives and traditions in the district
- Assessment of the level of acceptance of a new academic/curriculum leader
- Tolerance level of the staff and administrators for change
- Developing a support base through discussions with the superintendent's cabinet, union leadership, principals, curriculum supervisors, subject matter committees, departmental and special-needs staff, and parent advising committees

Curriculum Architects

It was important to consider the needs of and issues related to special education, ELL, gifted, and low-performing students and their differing cultures and backgrounds. Taking into account staff leadership needs for training and support was another consideration. The plan was devised to reorganize the central office curriculum staff to reflect responsibility for preK–12 supervision rather than elementary or secondary coordination. PreK–12 content teacher teams met to discuss needs and concerns about their disciplines. This staff involvement in the early stages encouraged ownership and empowerment in the decision-making process.

Secondary curriculum directors, supervisors, and coordinators selected a discipline to develop as a curriculum prototype. The coordinators sought to focus on secondary issues related to the items below:

- Acknowledging progress and discussions about the need for curriculum restructuring
- Solving long-standing curriculum problems
- Logically piloting a curriculum-adoption process through articulated efforts
- Becoming involved in the process

Curriculum supervisors and coordinators were requested to develop a process for selecting a team of teachers for curriculum writing. Curriculum and program staff, principals, teachers, union leaders, executive cabinet members, school board members, and the parent group leadership were asked to recommend curriculum writers. Recognizing that not every teacher is a curriculum writer or designer, specific qualities were sought for the curriculum architects. Criteria included identification of the following:

1. Teachers who were highly respected by their peers for their expertise in specific content knowledge, instructional practices, and consistent positive outcomes with various student populations
2. Teachers who represented the highest level of professionalism and were capable of modeling and communicating best practices to others
3. Teachers who had the interest and ability to work collaboratively and be open to new ideas and educational change
4. Teachers who were good leaders and had broad perspectives on educating students at different grade, school, ability, and content levels
5. Teachers who understood how to help the "weakest teachers" (this was an important characteristic that facilitated the philosophy that if the weakest teacher had the ability to understand the curriculum and its implementation, the chances were stronger for overall improved teaching and learning)
6. Teachers who had a successful record of teaching students of varied abilities

These teacher teams were included in summer curriculum writing. They were compensated for their time and work throughout the development period of four weeks. Research noted that the central task of improving schools was to define what students needed to know and be able to do. This included expanding the vision of what it meant to graduate successful students. The implementation of a coherent curriculum linked to successful instruction, resource interventions, and assessments often accomplishes this task.

DEEPER LEVELS OF KNOWLEDGE AND THINKING

The new curriculum organizational structure allowed K–12 content teams to discuss curriculum and instructional needs and issues across the school spectrum. Rather than specifying content alone, they advocated teaching fewer topics in greater depth through broadly stated concepts that students should master. To this end, the task of the preK–12 curriculum teams began. They met to draft a content curriculum framework for each discipline. Considerations included essential knowledge, overarching themes and concepts, generalizations, process (thinking) skills, and products to demonstrate knowledge and skills.

The teams worked in and across disciplines, thus achieving natural curriculum integration. Essential knowledge and skills were threaded throughout the disciplines. A pre-grade-12 content scope and sequence articulated broad essential concepts and enduring knowledge and questions for all disciplines and grade levels. Content and explicit curriculum would follow to guide grade-level expectations.

The curriculum was designed so that local needs could be met, yet preK–12 expectations would remain consistent within the larger context of the overarching themes and concepts. This was quite a paradigm shift for general education teachers. Using a deductive process or backward design theory created frustration and anxiety because the expected student outcomes drove the construction of the curriculum, starting from pre–grade 12 to prekindergarten. The articulated curriculum began to take shape to allow a full view of curriculum concepts and *nonnegotiable knowledge* at every grade level for every student.

Coherence and order to the delivery of instruction was beginning to take shape, which meant that the overfull curriculum was being addressed. Manageability was achieved by concentrating on prioritizing content standards, core content, and essential knowledge into three categories: *essential, important*, and *"nice to do."* The nice-to-do category often related to what teachers recognized as "doing one's own thing in the classroom." A second undergirding goal was to spend time identifying how to develop and determine what constituted good work based on standards of curriculum content, materials, and student supports, including technology and so forth.

Raising the Bar

The next step was to address higher-level thinking as a developmental component throughout. The teams developed "process scopes and sequences" that addressed how one thinks and uses, or processes, information. Common in gifted education curriculum, these require students not only to acquire advanced knowledge but also to use different, often higher-level, ways to question, think about, and communicate content and deep-level understanding.

Interdisciplinary or common skills across subject areas were sequenced into developmental thinking levels of difficulty. The thinking processes were categorized under four levels of instruction—introduce, develop, master, and reinforce—for four grade-level ranges (K–3, 4–6, 7–9, and 10–12). Process skills that are commonly used by elegant thinkers were addressed:

1. Creative thinking (brainstorm, formulate explore possibilities, generate)
2. Critical thinking (analyze, categorize, distinguish, contrast, evaluate)
3. Independent inquiry and research (self-directed learning, presearch plan, search, evaluate, justify)
4. Affective and psychomotor considerations (increase self-awareness, display flexibility, incorporate individual beliefs and values, manage personal emotions)
5. Recall, memory, and associative thinking (concentrate, practice, connect, remember, expand)

Each writing team selected a process skill and researched the literature to determine verbs to differentiate teaching, learning, and student performances of the specific skill. The first process skill, creativity, modeled the remainder of the design. Because this was a shift for most teachers, the process scope and sequence took more time, so the timeline for completion was expanded until the following year.

A *product* scope and sequence was also developed to define student performance indicators—the work or products produced by students that could measure tangible evidence of learning. Student products addressed the various intelligences and learning styles using different ways of knowing:

1. Verbal spoken (debate, develop questions, interview, survey, report, critique, analysis)
2. Verbal written (composition such as an essay, poem, or rap; community service plan)
3. Media and visual arts (video, website, chart, diagram, graph, display, computer program, spreadsheet)
4. Performing arts (singing, interpretative dance, storytelling, acting, songwriting, computer-assisted composition and recital, concerts, historical or cultural simulation)
5. Kinesthetic/psychomotor (use hands-on materials to demonstrate complex math concepts, rhythmic demonstration)

Identifying content and performance standards and benchmarks (checkpoints) for evaluation of learning was matched to content and performance indicators. Student products and work would assess the degree of understanding. Units of study aligned to essential knowledge and skills, and evidence-based interventions and instructional materials were the finishing pieces of the five year curriculum plan.

CHAPTER 8

Avoiding Internal Struggles and Pitfalls

There is nothing wrong with change, if it is in the right direction.

Winston Churchill

After the Everybody's School District writing teams finished the curriculum redesign as described in chapter 7, the real transformational work was to begin. To promote and receive feedback from principals and teachers, information was shared about the curriculum restructuring and frameworks in each school with department heads and subject matter committees in all disciplines. Organized school visitation teams consisting of volunteer teachers, principals, coordinators, and curriculum staff presented the framework drafts at staff meetings in all schools. The academic leader attended each presentation to reinforce the vision and the instructional leader role, to develop relationships, and to hear comments firsthand.

There was a noticeable change in the staff. The writing team became more adept at discussing the curriculum development efforts. As the presentations and conversations progressed, the teams became better at sharing plans for developing process and product scopes and sequences and assessment tools. They explained how the framework connected to work in the classroom and addressed concerns about "top-down" directives and feelings of intrusiveness for teachers who wanted to continue "doing their own thing." It was clear that the level of interest and involvement in the curriculum process had increased throughout the school district. But there were also attitudes that said, "This too shall pass!"

Overall, the writing teams were able to give staff enough information to determine progress. The content was consistent with general expectations. The writing team offered a coherent curriculum that incorporated integrated disciplines, high-order thinking, levels of difficulty (scaffolding) for varied learners to access common learning, inclusion of diverse cultural and learning considerations, and priorities for preK–12 teaching and learning.

Clearly, the district was in a transitional period of curriculum restructuring. Strategic planning had included widely represented group consensus on essential knowledge, objectives, and priorities. Critical analysis of curriculum and instructional strengths and weaknesses of students and teachers had been discussed. Goal congruence, ambiguity, and fragmentation had been addressed. To share with the public, a large replica of the framework was developed with color-coded, threaded concepts, knowledge, and skills throughout the grade and school levels to provide a visual diagram of the building blocks to learning.

Information was solicited from various stakeholders through focus group meetings, especially people from the business and industry sectors. The question posed to the groups was this: What do students from Everybody's School District need to know and be able to do when they graduate from high school? Participants brainstormed and identified skills. Then curriculum frameworks were reviewed to see if there were any significant omissions of critical expected outcomes suggested by external stakeholders.

As the writing teams received feedback, the frameworks were continually refined, redefined, and reevaluated. The process was delayed somewhat to ensure time for adequate staff and community input and ownership. Broad participation and consensus required participants to confront conflicts and opposing opinions. Stakeholders' input represented important feedback to the educators regarding sometimes differing but important beliefs and priorities for curriculum content and lifelong learning. Throughout the process, obstacles, attitudes, and roadblocks created barriers that impeded progress.

The key element was the facilitator or leader, who provided quality control and leadership techniques that pulled all the pieces together. Research supports the fact that successful change takes time—at least three to five years. By year 3, it became evident that a larger number of principals and teachers were ready, even eager, for a manageable ("doable") systemic curriculum. The paradigm shift had begun. The frameworks had provided readiness and preparation for developing common ground for learning, regardless of school program, student population, or teaching style. It was now time to shift to the grade-level specifics, which would provide accountability for teachers and parents.

EVALUATING THE IMPACT

Drafting the frameworks provided the scaffolding necessary to define the concrete, grade-level specific skills and knowledge that was appropriate for the weakest teacher and the weakest student. The curriculum writers moved to developing levels of difficulty to suit the needs of learners who were capable of learning more complex content. Because the vision and the big picture had preceded the development of the parts, this process did not incur the strong resistance between and across disciplines and grade levels that had marked earlier work.

The initial scopes and sequences provided the bridge to the paradigm shift and cooperation needed to coordinate and standardize district curriculum. The overarching themes and concepts were widely referred to during the development of local school curriculum components. Spiraling effects of the restructuring efforts ultimately expanded into a pilot project for social studies/history, which was the first completed discipline. As the first stage of development, the pilot represented a degree of success.

There was a quantum leap made by teachers of grades 7–12 from a ten-year "war zone" atmosphere to the delivery of an agreed-upon, cohesive curriculum. This was the first controversial discipline in terms of resistance to defining a district standard. Once completed, the social studies curriculum became the model that demonstrated potential for successful change. This was largely due to the knowledge and cooperative team leadership of the social studies curriculum coordinator. Upon completion of the social studies curriculum frameworks and grade-level expectations, work began to align with classroom strategies, materials, and resources.

Overall, the restructuring process was long and difficult. It might be compared to childbirth—painful, but with anticipation of joyous results. Signs of the impending "birth" surfaced through increased attention to preK–12 standards-based curriculum development. Other effects of the curriculum restructuring efforts noted are listed below:

- There was increased discussion and development of K–12 curricula.
- Many teachers and parents indicated that they were relieved to see a systematic approach to common outcomes, in light of local school decision-making trends.
- Incorporating large numbers of teachers as curriculum designers gave them aligned training and professional development opportunities.
- Individual disciplines maintained their dignity, while at the same time serving as a vehicle for interdisciplinary learning.
- Instruction was concentrated on the most essential (nonnegotiable) knowledge in each discipline, making the curriculum more manageable. (There was more work that could be done in this area with requirements to teach more and more.)

MORE IMPACTS

The stage was set for more educational change. These experiences laid the foundation for the following:

- Future decisions relevant to instruction based on articulated expected district-wide goals and learning outcomes (budget, resources, technology, media, student information and learning systems, site-based efforts, assessment tools, and new initiatives such as RtI).
- Allowing updates and site-based work to continue using the dynamic curriculum as the roadmap.
- Articulating curriculum that could provide equitable access to content, processes, and products.
- Linking special education, English-language-learner, gifted/talented, career/technical education, remedial, prevention/intervention, and other academic and student support programs to general curriculum as the foundation.
- Expansion, extensions, modifications, accommodations, and differentiation of the essential curriculum to maximize the potential of all students.
- Teachers addressing their own professional development in the context of the new educational environment that was created. Training of teacher trainers, mentors, and coaches were strategies used to start the development process of helping teachers create a curriculum plan specific to subject areas, grade levels, school sites, and specified teacher and leader needs.

PLANNING TO MAKE CHANGE HAPPEN: THE PAYOFF

We often complain about the number of changes, but educational change can happen. We must redefine what we are *not* in the business of doing. We must select priorities and show very strong effort and improvement in those areas. Educational change manifests itself in new materials, new behaviors, new beliefs, and new understandings. Change is a learning process. It is difficult because it concerns individuals.

The curriculum design model above demonstrated that schools and school districts can show examples of successful change and can begin to institute new insights. Deliberate change can be brought about through processes and procedures that are carefully and diligently managed by an effective leader who understands the educational landscape.

The developmental nature of the process required rigorous mental exercises, which provided a prototype for determining significant and topical learning. Curriculum guidance began to radiate outward in all directions and flow to all levels. Gains were hard fought and won. Cooperative teaming and the beginning of an atmosphere that promoted a free exchange of information and ideas started to surface. Priorities were generated through difficult negotiation and consensus, and a district-wide vision was identified.

Classroom activities began to link to the new curriculum. Fragmentation and segmentation were minimized. Order started to surface from the chaos of the overcrowded curriculum. As the curriculum efforts unfolded, the reality of engaging all children in high levels of learning held great potential for ringing true. Educational efforts supplied the catalyst for providing substance to the creed "All children have potential to learn if given opportunity and access to thoughtful, purposeful knowledge."

UNEXPECTED OUTCOMES

The curriculum redesign process started with a vision that was developed and accomplished. The curriculum redesign process started with the vision for all teachers to become:

1. informed and knowledgeable about the essential knowledge expected of all students;
2. well versed in essential knowledge and systemic, comprehensive core curriculum expectations;
3. engaged in extensive professional development on core content learning standards and strategies; and
4. able to effectively match interventions, materials, and technologies needed for instruction to improve and increase learning for all students.

It ended with outcomes far beyond expectations.

Stimulation of creativity on the part of teachers illustrated how real educational change can inspire and improve teacher practice. Unexpected outcomes resulted from the critical analysis of curriculum and instructional strengths and weaknesses, addressing goal congruence, ambiguity, and segmentation of teacher's efforts. Cases in point are listed below:

1. Some teachers reported that they enrolled in master's degree programs to develop multicultural and special education lessons and resources for concepts included in the curriculum framework. Lessons were developed and evaluated for quality components and included in a portal for district-wide sharing.
2. A high school teacher proposed a "school within a school" that became a model for an integrated program based on the curriculum framework.

3. Health and physical education teachers restructured to a preK–10 program structure, thus leaving room in the curriculum for other priorities. The feeling was that a lifestyle of health, nutrition, and wellness needed to be solidified in the curriculum by the time students completed tenth grade. In addition, a teacher who was not on the curriculum writing team grasped the concepts to the extent that a new course was proposed based on the curriculum frameworks.
4. The Secondary Review Curriculum Committee (comprised of secondary teachers from each discipline) proposed procedural changes to align with curriculum and framework changes.
5. A teacher wrote an article in a professional science journal relating the experiences of a curriculum writer and the development of the discipline.
6. A career/technical education teacher proposed eliminating repetitions in career/technical education courses matched to general education curriculum expectations.
7. Coordinators for math, English/language arts, and media services requested additional curriculum framework development for their disciplines.
8. Staff development was adjusted to enhance learning for highly capable and struggling students in the general classrooms, as well as other special-needs students.
9. A grant was requested to provide funds for implementing performance assessment and developing implementation and measurements for process and product skills for all students.
10. Local school and district staff development content began to focus on encouraging teachers to bring learning objectives, lessons, activities, culminating projects, textbooks, and other related resources to collaborate on how to approach content standards and the curriculum frameworks from thematic, interdisciplinary, and real-world perspectives.

Activities such as these show the spiraling effects that curriculum restructuring can have and the opportunities that can offer students stronger educational experiences before the need for interventions. Parts of the curriculum framework may need modifications from time to time; however, more of significance was accomplished than "tinkering around the edges of the curriculum and restructuring process." Now it was possible to focus on procedural or technical aspects, such as class scheduling, team teaching, apprenticeships, interventions, and developmental appropriateness.

THIS TOO SHALL PASS—OR WILL IT?

The new frameworks represented the potential for students to have high-quality instruction that did not focus on specific learning activities or interventions. The focus had shifted to how activities and other elements connected to the learning continuum from kindergarten through grade 12.

The change process and levels of concern will always have to be addressed on a continual basis. Questions and objections might take the form of:

- "How does this relate to my classroom?"
- "What activities will I teach?"
- "Why are the district frameworks needed when we are engaged in site-based management?"
- "I've been teaching for 25 years—if it ain't broke, don't fix it!"
- "This is too abstract."
- "I just need a simple skills continuum. I don't understand all of this. My students don't need all of this anyway."
- "Why do we have to have a consistent format?"
- "This does not serve my individual purpose."

Educational change efforts must involve teachers in decision-making. If all students have access to the same knowledge at different levels of difficulty, then differences become issues of instructional practice rather than curriculum content. The goal of developing higher-level thinking, curriculum, and achievement must be solidified with appropriate training and preparation for both teachers and students. Future questions may focus on adequate funding, instructional resources, data-gathering methods, conflicting philosophies, and assessment and evaluation of student learning. In reference to RtI, evidenced interventions will need to be matched to curriculum expectations at various levels of intensity in an RtI framework.

The end result is to ensure access to challenging and enriching curriculum. For the academic leader, the end product must be provision for support and advocacy for improving the quality of instruction that will measurably increase student achievement for all student populations. The true test of a good curriculum is whether it is used by classroom teachers or whether it is "business as usual." In-service sessions following the curriculum development demonstrated that many teachers-in-training used the curriculum framework documents to match proposed expectations for increasing standards and rigor for all students.

Radiating outward, the result should be a more appropriate educational experience for all district students. If teacher performance improves, students reap the benefits. As Response to Intervention continues to grow, like most new school endeavors, its survival rests on understanding the complex, difficult work. Shortcuts and easy answers are most likely doomed to failure.

As demonstrated in the detailed comprehensive curriculum design process of Everybody's School District, the ability of RtI or any innovative educational improvement effort to succeed is directly proportionate to creating opportunity and time for understanding the processes, procedures, and changes. By placing focus on the role of the development of curriculum, the goal of enlightening and instructing professional educators to promote a more coherent approach to teaching and learning can be attained.

CHAPTER 9

Queries and Opportunities

Knowledge comes from taking things apart, but wisdom comes from putting things together.

John A. Morrison

Response to Intervention is mandated in some states and districts, and optional or nonexistent in others. Adequate numbers of teachers and specialists are not available to address the multiple needs of students in certain schools and districts. RtI calls for individual instruction and teacher judgment based on evidence-based decisions, and therefore results across various school types and student populations can vary based on differences in teacher factors.

There are models of success, but evidence-based research is minimal. Adoption rates are growing, yet no one has figured out how to identify and evaluate interventions in a comprehensive, sustained manner across classrooms and schools. Screening, monitoring, and diagnostic tools have to be better defined. Some of the floating questions about RtI are listed below:

1. What are the best measures for predicting learning problems?
2. How can exit standards, high-stakes benchmarks, graduation standards, and learning standards be aligned with RtI procedures?
3. How can teachers manage the RtI process during the instructional day, especially if they are responsible for large numbers of underperforming students?
4. What are the proven models and interventions that are most successful in inner cities and rural environments?

Even though there are questions and dilemmas, it only makes sense that the first requirement is to ensure that a student's learning is initially linked to adequate school and classroom instruction. There are many preconditions and mediating factors that need to be considered. Undertaking educational renewal is a tedious commitment requiring steadfastness, tolerance, knowledge, and skill. To facilitate a defensible end point, the following precautions and recommendations are offered for consideration.

1. Ensure that a systemic, coherent curriculum model is in place. Deciding what knowledge is essential is an important prerequisite for making intervention decisions. Teachers need a solid plan of curriculum and instruction. They need time to implement large-scale improvement based on informed understanding and improvement. Consider the extent to which a comprehensive district curriculum is aligned and doable across disciplines. Determine if the curriculum provides the opportunity for all students to access essential knowledge. Determine how core curriculum can be modified appropriately in the context of general education. Teachers need to link instructional strategies, resources, and then interventions to help students reach full potential.

2. Align resources, including human. Funding support and limitations must be clearly established. Any endeavor involves a great amount of time, which translates to money. After a clear picture has been established, it must be converted to hours, resources, and personnel costs. The demands of funding new initiatives, in some cases, can be almost as trying as purchasing intervention programs or materials. A district must make a commitment to maintain an adequate discretionary RtI budget for a three- to five-year program.

Funding sources need to be identified across school and district funds. Interventions must be prioritized based on evaluative data matched to the understanding of the effects of interventions on outcomes for individual students.

Realizing that schools may not have the financial resources to provide all services, creative ways are needed to align resources to provide services to students and families. An example is a "one-stop shop" where students and families access social, health, medical, recreation, family, and educational support before and after school, on weekends and holidays, and during extended hours aligned with family work schedules.

Educators and policymakers must understand the relationship between how money is spent and how staff and time are used. If policy- and decision-makers are serious about moving children forward, equitable funding and staffing must be allocated so that schools can provide staff and service providers in every school.

3. Teaching and learning must be strategic. Rethink the practice of placing struggling learners in classrooms taught by inexperienced teachers. Ill-prepared teachers often lack experience and knowledge for determining what interferes with the teaching and learning process. Accountability pressures that focus on narrow definitions of curriculum and learning must be rethought.

Beginning in kindergarten, teachers can usually identify students who are "behind" in school-related skills as soon as they enter the classroom—children who cannot recognize their name, the child who uses very little vocabulary, or the child who pushes and shoves other children while at play. Children who display a lack of preparedness must be identified early and provided appropriate opportunities to function with peers in the school environment.

4. Organize for effective instruction, prevention, and intervention. Carefully plan RtI initiatives, and take into account considerations that might affect teachers, students, and families. Avoid the "smorgasbord effect." Beware of the "research-based," "standards-aligned," and "evidence-based" labels. Most resources and instructional materials do not have long-standing evidence. There must be a distinction between an intervention that has been tested for subject matter content validity and the intervention itself.

Align with curriculum expectations, and develop strong criteria for selecting interventions. New initiatives and school reform adoptions must be taken in incremental steps. Research must be expanded on programs and strategies and best theories to practice applied across various school levels, contexts, and student populations. Proven interventions that address specific academic concerns; intervention intensities; culture, language, behavior, and socioeconomic levels; and disability types are needed.

5. Acknowledge the realities of today's classroom. General education teachers are responsible for all children assigned to them. For some classrooms, this can mean that more than 90 percent of students who are at risk due to the many in- and out-of-school factors that negatively impact school performance. RtI can be very threatening to some, and overwhelming to others, because of the numerous reform efforts thrust upon teachers.

Secondary schools and classrooms are the recipients of years of school failure and accumulated student frustration with learning. Reform models for instructional improvement must take these realities into consideration. If RtI is to drive measurable learning, a good starting point is to help adults through the progressive stages of learning. The evolution of change and transition must be an integral part of the development and implementation process.

Nothing succeeds like success. Recognition of work and its worth generates enthusiasm and energy. Many teachers operate on a concrete, traditional level. It may be too much of a shift to operate with a new, dramatically different approach to instruction for various students. The paradox is, how can we expect students to abruptly master higher-level concepts and thinking if most teachers and other adults have difficulty shifting from old paradigms to connect pieces into an overall picture?

6. Teacher preparation and skill matters. Since test scores are the main measure of school success, it must be noted that disparities across teacher abilities, school district types, schools, classrooms, years of experience, and teacher preparation must be minimized. Quality teachers encourage, inspire, engage, reflect, monitor, and guide in different ways. Teaching is not a simple matter; therefore, teachers need to graduate from rigorous teacher preparation with appropriate skills in place matched to local school district needs. This will require an aligned, seamless understanding and transition from universities to classrooms in school districts. It will be difficult for higher education to align with local districts if some commonality of curriculum, materials, and initiatives is not achieved.

Schools and districts have to refrain from asking teachers to "stop drowning while learning to swim." Most teachers cannot process innovative practices along with the day-to-day teaching responsibilities. Strategic ways are needed to introduce RtI process to teachers, perhaps in phases, so they will not be as overwhelmed. Teacher/leader preparation and training programs must be developed in partnership with school districts. College and university presidents and professors must help determine and negotiate how to meaningfully prepare teachers for the realities of the work.

7. Identify and train teachers to implement interventions with fidelity. We know that some students need interventions. Through investigation, we must determine how to best manage fidelity assurance and assess the value of interventions in terms of types and evidence. A more urgent emphasis must be placed on research and program evaluation to determine which interventions and programs work under which conditions. We also need to know how standards-based curriculum content and assessments are aligned to interventions and instruction.

There must be a stronger bridge between special and general educators. Fidelity to instruction and interventions cannot be widely assessed until teachers have time, knowledge, and ability to effectively implement RtI processes and contribute accurate data on the quality of instruction and student learning.

8. Teachers need time to meet and plan. Teachers must discuss, reexamine, and work collaboratively to focus on the strengths and weaknesses of individual students. Time must be provided for general and special education teachers, content specialists, and related service providers to strategize, diagnose, and develop appropriate learning plans for students. In addition, teachers need time to review and understand mounds of data that are available, link data to instructional decision-making, and monitor student progress and learning.

9. Develop models for secondary education. It is common knowledge that reading is the precursor to academic success in all subject areas and across the content areas. A few school districts are beginning to explore RtI models for kindergarten through grade 12. Generally there is a critical need to identify secondary-school-level, evidence-based interventions that remediate and accelerate reading, language, writing, and math development.

Until effective approaches are identified and schools are resourced with reading specialists and the like, secondary school students will continue to struggle with meeting grade-level, subject-area, and proficiency targets. High school teachers need massive retraining to change the process of instruction to meet varying needs of students in various courses, subject areas, and lessons.

Understanding how to manage the RtI process using traditional or alternative schedules for class periods and subject areas is an example of training that is needed. In this time of shrinking budgets, resources, and staff, there is no need to reinvent the wheel, search for something that is in vogue, or seek the next innovation. Identifying such models can help lead the way to selecting interventions and frameworks for improving learning conditions.

10. Anticipate unexpected problems and concerns. Potential problems might involve parents who take litigious action on compliance, due-process, and special-education procedures. Some parents/guardians or advocates may feel that the RtI process takes too long to make determinations when there is a threat of a disability. Educators must be prepared for questions about timeliness of referrals for special education services. They are also advised to steer clear of using RtI as a reason to avoid or delay referrals for special education or English-language-learner services.

If there is a sense that a child has a disability backed up with clear evidence, parental consultation and involvement, and reliable documentation, a child should not go through the steps of the RtI process. Policies must be in place to clarify and evaluate RtI procedures so that everyone has a clear understanding of how they relate to special education laws and rules (Weatherly, 2008).

Also, it might be wise to strategize how to handle leadership shifts that occur in the middle of an RtI implementation or any renewal process. Principals and district leadership are unstable in many school districts; therefore, a contingency plan may come in handy for unexpected occurrences that could impede the momentum of addressing students' needs.

11. Family, community, and university support are critical. A child's opportunities and success have a lot to do with his or her out-of-school experiences. We know that there are disparities in those experiences based on family income. But it is clear that these conditions cannot be used as excuses for schools not taking responsibility for their part in the educational process.

Families, schools, and communities also have a duty to partner with schools in support of student success.

Effective collaborations and partnerships between schools and mental health, law enforcement, public health, social, youth, and family service agencies; community and faith organizations; higher education institutions; professional organizations; and others must be identified to help support vulnerable students and families. Schools cannot solve or respond to all societal, family, and community problems that interfere with learning.

Educators must seek and coordinate stronger federal, state, community, industry, and family wraparound services that address out-of-school student needs. A nonacademic agency could add a more holistic picture of a student's functioning in different settings.

Philip Jackson (2010, p. 2), executive director of the Chicago-based Black Star Project, made the following observation:

> While educators, society and government all have a role, it must be acknowledged that parents, families and communities of these youths hold the key. A national infrastructure must be created to manage the resources, programs, ideas and people who can solve this problem. Programs and good intentions cannot fix this problem. The solution needs to be comprehensive, systemic, well conceived, well funded, and well executed. The best school safety solutions start in homes and communities. The best discipline plan for a child is a cultural framework of mutual respect and self-discipline taught at a young age by their parents and the communities in which they live. The best mentors are loving, nurturing and caring parents.

12. Employ technology. Tools and resources are needed to alleviate some of the cumbersome administrative paperwork and time-intensive requirements. In addition, technology is needed as a longitudinal tracking system for gathering data on individual student growth. Data collection and reporting processes for special education and RtI should be seamless.

Training and development must be accomplished in small steps with time to practice each step in the classroom. Training has to be backed up with high levels of support and aligned to the needs of multiple users and the challenges teachers face.

Conversely, technologies can be inhibiting barriers if they are not integrated across purposes. Data must be accurate and secure enough to accommodate variations in processes, forms, selected interventions, and procedures. Parent portals can enhance two-way communication and ongoing educational planning between schools, parents, teachers, and students.

Technology, however, is only as good as the user, who inputs data either correctly or inaccurately and may or may not use the special features designed to advance learning. It is helpful to pay attention to maintenance and upgrades to keep the technology working. Some school districts are better equipped than others. Equitable funding and access for robust infrastructure, Internet, and dedicated administrative and instructional technologies for anywhere, anytime use continues to be a need for many states, cities, and school districts. Technical assistance, upgrades, and teacher/staff training will be ongoing needs.

CHAPTER 10

Transitioning to Schools and Classrooms of the Future

SEARETHA SMITH-COLLINS AND JACOB E. COLLINS

We live in the present, we dream of the future, and we learn eternal truths from the past.

Madame Chiang Kai-Shek

Public education is being redefined by a collective body of endeavors that have evolved by creating new elements and innovations. Public education is constantly changing in unpredictable ways. There is the absence of an evolutionary process for large-scale use. Because innovations are evolving over time, there is no identifiable theory of progression that can provide consistency and encourage planning in teaching routines.

After years of time and millions of dollars invested in changes in education such as the technology revolution, schools still have not been able to grasp the full means to integrate technology into classrooms. Perhaps along with the innovation, the lacking piece is knowledge of the innovators to understand and know how to marry the new tools with the implicit knowledge of how to implement the craft of teaching. As a result, oftentimes new solutions offer predicaments instead of possibilities.

Today we have access to what reflects multidimensional learning and more understanding of the human brain than ever before. Some might say it is the best of times, others that it is the worst of times. It is a time for embracing teaching and collaborating with all who have a genuine interest in providing a democratic public education for all. It is a time to reexamine and identify what has been working over time, and perhaps to revisit traditional operating principles that need revitalizing.

For those who might feel it is the worst of times, the focus is on current attempts to influence new definitions of public education that favor privatization and corporate interest. There is no agreement on motives, processes, or who should lead and transform schooling. The time is overdue for policy- and decision-makers to reflect realistically on what has changed in current society that can be countered in the educational setting, and which things are beyond the scope and responsibility of schools to handle.

Political and financial agendas, new governance structures, and experimental practices have been imposed on urban schools to spark what is considered "innovation" and competition in the public school marketplace. This is not a new phenomenon. Tomorrow's classrooms and schools have always been a vision of something better. Some have envisioned something far into the future, which in essence would be the terminal phase in the evolutionary process of school and classrooms. Others have designed solutions to give a final answer to the elusive challenge of transforming public education.

In the attempt to structure a view and lens through which we might predict public education and schools in the future, it might be useful to reflect and consider other "firsts" during periods that were thought to be revolutionary educational changes at the time. As we proceed into the digital age, which has indeed been revolutionary, let's take the innovation of technology in schools as the example. We in fact can readily say that the evolution of computer-related technology and attempts to integrate it into instruction have evolved immensely. Yet today, fully integrating the use of technology is still a challenge for many educators.

School districts across the nation can look back over two decades to harness the best features of computer-related technology for classroom use. Briefly, it all started in 1984 when schools started installing thousands of Apple II; IBM 8880, 286–486, and PS/2-series; Commodore 64; Amigo; and Mac-series desktop computers. These systems were the first and evolved over time, making steady progress in the twentieth century with the introduction of hard drives, more storage, connectivity, and networking.

It was yet another revolution when the CD-ROM was introduced in Atlanta by IBM with much fanfare, when the curtains were pulled back and a PC version of Louis Armstrong's "What a Wonderful World" stimulated a standing ovation from technologists and educators looking toward the future. They saw the next development that would bring yet another transformation into the classroom with 600-megabyte CD-ROMs holding lesson content loaded with voice and video for the first time. Dr. Martin Luther King Jr.'s and President John F. Kennedy's speeches were quickly moved from the old laser discs to this new platform. At the same time, CD-ROMs increased storage capacity and became the primary source of lessons designed as state of the art at the time.

During this same period, it is useful to remember that the U.S. Congress established the Office of Technology Assessment in 1984. Billions of dollars were provided to states and local districts to develop and implement technology plans. The U.S. Department of Education sponsored model grants for colleges and universities to work with school districts to conduct research and develop models for others to replicate. One of their major works in conjunction with the eRate Act of 1994 and 1996 culminated in a document called "POWER ON: New Tools for Teachers" (NETS) for use of technology in the classroom. As one research effort among many, Apple did a decade-long study of technology infusion and compiled the nationally known Apple Classrooms of Tomorrow (ACOT) study.

All of these efforts were exciting and terrific innovations for the twentieth century. However, as we fast forward, we are still looking for the "classroom of the future" for the twenty-first century. We can agree that computers are now a part of the background scene, along with electronic whiteboards, cell phones, iPods, iPads, gaming tools, laptops and notebooks, global positioning systems, Facebook, Web pages, virtual learning, smartphones, cloud computing, texting, tweeting, and Skyping. All are part of the platform, information, and communication systems through which instruction is delivered and managed. They are the new and emerging tools for continuing growth in the digital age, with students being comfortable with almost any digital tool. Yet today, we still strive to provide equitable technological access throughout America's schools where innovation has not necessarily modified the learning environment as expected. This continues to be a part of the equity agenda.

We must understand the significance of these shifts and help produce learning to foster environments that enable teachers to be more successful in this constantly developing new age. Planners and decision-makers must understand the organizational conditions and needs for managing the implementation of classroom policies, procedures, tools, and ongoing support.

During the 1980s and 1990s, many futurists predicted that evolution of classroom instruction would emerge with the onset of computer-based education (CBE) and computer-assisted technology (CAT). It was expected that, with the new technologies, teacher workloads would be reduced and costs would be lessened due to the need for fewer teachers in classrooms. Today, the same concept has evolved with idea that online learning, the wave of the twenty-first century, will reduce the cost of education and potentially replace the need for teachers in the future. Sometimes, it appears that educational reform is like a dog chasing its tail around in circles.

We have learned that instructional technology in the classroom can provide broad access to curriculum and facilitates interest and learning for self-directed learners. But not all students respond to online learning, so it should be offered as merely another option for instruction. We know that students must have the requisite skills and dispositions for online learning. We also know that teacher relationships are one of the strongest factors in the success of disadvantaged learners and that online teachers cannot provide the level of communication, monitoring, and motivation to sustain the learning of students who are in jeopardy.

Struggling students often do not have the background knowledge, skills, and experience to adequately progress through online curriculum without the help and support of a teacher. Learners who are challenged depend on a teacher to respond, facilitate, and make adjustments, including one-to-one, small-group, and "old school" direct or straightforward teaching supplementing lessons with print and nonprint resources. In fact, if a teacher is not available to help when needed, chances are greater that students will reach their frustration level or just give up.

Online learning alone is not for everyone. However, for those students who can readily benefit from virtual learning, it can be a great opportunity. It is useful for self-directed learners who feel a sense of control over their learning and usually do not need much facilitation from teachers. Again, balance in approaches is needed to provide the right options for the right students. For some, a real-time teacher will always be needed, and lessons over time have demonstrated that need.

We need to assemble the most powerful research-based principles and build appropriate combinations of instructional strategies, innovations, technologies, and school transformation theories. A clear plan for how curriculum, instruction, materials, interventions, teacher development, technology, and organizational support can be clarified and productively used is needed. The plan should ensure that innovations, solutions, and responses mediate and accommodate knowledge and understanding.

TEACHING THIS GENERATION OF STUDENTS

Table 1 provides a quick view of emerging trends and opportunities that must be addressed as schools move from the twentieth century to interacting with metacognitive (awareness of one's own knowledge) and cognitive (ways of knowing) processes operating in the minds of twenty-first-century students. Many have proposed solutions to the challenge of educating today's students, and continue to do so. The table summarizes some of the best thinking of the shifting needs of students in classrooms today

Table 1.   Understanding Today's Digital Student

Students from Previous Generations	Today's Digital-Age Students
Passive communicators	Hypercommunicators
Single taskers	Multitaskers
Work oriented	Play oriented
Linear thinking	Random access
Nonrelevancy learning	Learning must be relevant and fun
Single-sensory input	Multisensory input
Test-based first	Digital and graphics first
Reality-based learning	Fantasy-based learning
Conventional speed	Twitch speed

Adapted by Jacob Collins from G. Shelly, T. Cashman, R. Gunter, & G. Gunter, *Teachers Discovering Computers: Integrating Technology and Digital Media in the Classroom*, 5th ed. (Boston: Thomson/ Course Technology, 2008).

Knowing with certainty how to address these new learners as well as those who have historically struggled to learn is the real work of educational reform for the twenty-first century. It is important to remember that not all learners are multitaskers; in fact, perhaps more research is needed in that area. Are all students who are multitaskers and random learners able to focus, process, and sequence information when needed, or does this present learning difficulties for some? Do some learners need to learn at a conventional or even slower pace? Is there a point when play-oriented learning must be translated into work-oriented learning? These are questions that provide balance to new-age thinking that warrants not eliminating the good along with the bad.

Certainly we must consider the transitions that are needed to address today's shifts, but we must think about how to make adaptations that facilitate learning for varied students. There are certain in-class conditions that can mediate learning to decrease challenges to learning and help perpetuate performance and achievement, including the following:

- Add information to clarify or extend understanding.
- Target a much easier concept.
- Assign less to do.
- Make lessons more active and multisensory (verbal, visual, and tactile).
- Make concepts more concrete and tangible, such as using an interactive whiteboard or other digital resources.
- Enlarge materials, add color, and use graphic organizers and technology.
- Use small-group, personal instruction.
- Change the engagement strategy (make it fun and game-like, if appropriate).
- Target vocabulary that requires background knowledge, meaning, and vocabulary.

- Target general knowledge that needs to be taught.
- Make comparisons to bring meaning (include cultural examples, past and present and out-of-school experiences).
- Target omissions and gaps by stressing the expected sequence of content development (determine what skills are to be targeted, such as fractions or decimals).
- Build concepts and vocabulary (identify "big ideas" and common concepts and themes [e.g., forest, trees, plants]).
- Make performances less complex and use assistive technology and resources.

Perhaps we have finally arrived at the point in this evolutionary process where all of the salient components of the next generation of efforts are structured in just the right order, on the right pathway. This includes progressing in intuitive and scientific approaches and allowing teachers and schools time for identifying workable solutions for dealing with low performance. Teachers need implicit and explicit knowledge of what to use and how to use it as a part of the routine of teaching. They need to unconditionally know how to implement their craft and how to deal with parameters and breakdowns in the process.

Many of the new approaches have been specifically designed with very little input from teachers, principals, superintendents, students, and parents. Some of the new improvement efforts are billed through polished marketing strategies, movies, sound bites, television talk shows, and tsunami-like emphasis to reflect best hopes for a system of educational change. The crucial question is, what level of expertise should be required for anyone who proposes to have "a solution" that could affect the constancy of effort?

One of the reasons why most innovations fail is that teachers and leaders do not know with certainty how to implement the innovation or incorporate it with confidence into their craft. Most innovators think they know how to train teachers to implement a solution, but this is actually where the most serious shortcomings occur. Most efforts fall short of helping teachers develop the consistency and follow-through needed to evolve into routine teaching. This can account for much of the explanation of why instructional technology, for example, has never fully penetrated the classroom. The answer lies in flawed theories of the means to the end and a flawed understanding of the conditions, science, and craft of teaching.

THE MORAL IMPERATIVE

In another revolutionary area, various people are troubleshooting teacher preparation and development of the "brightest and best" teachers. Again, the means to the end may be a bit flawed. We must be sure to include those who represent the faces and cultures of the various student populations. We are witnessing the disappearing act of:

1. experienced teachers and leaders of color;
2. a balance of male and female teachers and leaders;
3. educators who are over the age of forty;
4. teachers who are willing to work more than three years in the profession to develop a level of expertise;
5. teachers with the fortitude and ethics to maintain the high ideals of the profession; and
6. teachers who are truly trained and prepared to teach with skill and enjoyment over time.

Quick-fix leader and teacher preparation programs do not provide the forums and time for the prerequisite work needed for successful, deep-rooted change in teaching and leading. The recent calls for more and more rigor come without the proper preparation that one expects of professionals in a field. For example, we would most likely not knowingly get on an airplane with a novice pilot or trust our life to an inexperienced surgeon! There are certain professionals that most people prefer have as much experience as possible so that unanticipated occurrences are met by prior knowledge and expertise. Teaching is one of those fields. Yet certain students are confronted with a similar educational experience, with far too many novice teachers in classroom with the most needy students.

Public education is committed to equity, and central to the creation of human caring is diversity within democracy. As a moral imperative and civil right in America, all students are entitled to the best education possible, with wide exposure to a diverse workforce of teachers and leaders. There was a hard-fought battle to ensure that students of color had significant numbers of role models in classrooms as teachers, in schools and districts as leaders, and elsewhere. Fulfilling this very imperative is among the crucial issues confronting public education across the nation, especially in the urban sector.

The problems are multifaceted, and the real school crisis lies in whether or not all Americans are provided access and opportunity for participation in an open society. Individuals should have the proficiencies to fully participate without regard to ethnicity, race, culture, gender, or social class differences. We are making progress, but we are not there by a long shot.

In an open society, all cultures and ethnic groups would be respected as legitimate participants, and the laws that "pamper the rich and impoverish the poor" would become nonexistent. In other words, there would not be a sense of blurred vision, whereby some are boxed in segregated demographics and extreme inequities or left out as have-nots (Kozol, 2010), while others (the haves) possess the view of progress and opportunities based on the benefits of accumulated wealth with access to the "good life" and quality schools.

These factors constitute the disparities in access to in- and out-of-school experiences that influence academic and background knowledge and life experiences for school readiness and progression. Such differences constitute the greatest alterable inequity separating students who live in or near poverty or who are raised with linguistic, racial, socioeconomic, and ability differences. I am primarily describing the conditions of many children from Latino, African American, Native American, and low-income families who suffer the most from the injustice of public education, as it currently exists.

CHAPTER 11

Lessons Learned: Bringing Order
to the Potential for Chaos

Education that brings about no change is as effective as a parachute that opens on the first bounce.

Anonymous

This leads to my final recommendation: *Bring order to the potential for chaos in public education.* Schools have operated as loosely coupled organizations with disconnected or inconsistent educational and curriculum goals, outcomes, and disparate opportunities for students. The previous chapters demonstrated that many schools and agencies are working toward correcting many of the predicaments and injustices that have surfaced over time. Moving into the present, the aim has shifted to being more decisive, deliberate, and defining about scientific-evidenced structures and processes for improving student outcomes.

Implementing any new initiative or innovation similar to Response to Intervention calls for a delicate mix of identifying possible student learning disabilities, correctly interpreting student achievement data, and creating an individual learning plan. Then teaching and learning must be monitored by all to make sure it works. The process must be duplicated and personalized for every student. "This is taxing work, and the hope is to avoid false steps" (*Scholastic Administrator*, 2009, p. 1).

As many schools across the nation try to maintain momentum and create recipes for developing basic and high-level knowledge and proficiency, what is most promising is that the education community is embracing a philosophy that can potentially change practice and lead to improved learning. RtI is one example of how schools are taking active responsibility for the learning of children and broadening their view of teaching and learning.

I believe that school leaders should drive change. It takes more than reading a book or going to a summer session to understand the implicit knowledge of how to deal with the values, the evolution of what has already been tried, and the embedded knowledge that is needed to move everyone forward. After several decades of improving "beacon of lighthouse" schools and districts, leaders should take charge to figure out how to spur success for the greater majority of schools and classrooms.

Improvements in public education cannot be based on lighthouse schools here and there. That has been the case for the past decades. Judgment of models of success cannot be based on a few successful charter or public schools or a small number of choice schools or strategies that do not represent the full spectrum of students who attend public schools. We have always had successful public school magnet and other innovative programs here and there across the nation, and there are numerous high-performing, functioning school systems across the country.

The real test is to examine entire large public school systems that have had the responsibility for all programs and students and that managed to significantly move the needle for its diverse students. This is where we should examine the scalable funding, organizational structures, leadership and teacher craft, unique characteristics, innovations, and outcomes. Then we must repeat and nurture the uniqueness of each system to help bring them to similar levels of equitable progress. These are the newsworthy places that we need to identify, research, define, and document their evolutionary process for bringing public education to large scale. This cannot be accomplished through trial balloons, instability, and experiments. We need sound practices for valid results.

Educators must collaboratively and collectively struggle with the dilemmas of how schools can reach a high level of efficiency, productivity, and responsiveness to change. Although there are needs for reform in most fields, perhaps there are valuable lessons that can be gained by studying strategic planning and parallel models in business and industry.

PARALLEL MODELING

It has been said that strategic planning is a process that helps organizations envision their future. Also, it has been said that in business, it helps to develop the necessary procedures and operations to achieve that future. Strategically identifying goals and achieving targets are complicated processes, especially when one sets goals and targets for learning. It has been documented over and over that the substance of day-to-day instructional decisions (what is taught), instructional strategies (the way it is taught), the school context and learning environment, the cultural understandings, resources, and preparation of the teachers are significant in determining how well students learn. Again, a major question surfaces: How can teachers provide the best education for each child?

When business and industry practices are analyzed, one usually finds they stick to what works to make a goal. Bits and pieces that depart from the main mission are not tolerated. In other words, business and industry maintain a focus. This has not been the case in educational practice.

Using the construction industry as a model, a design and foundation are provided. When a housing or building model is productive, modifications and adjustments are made here and there, but the basic structure that preserves the models usually remains. There are times when a new model is needed due to changes in homeowner and time period demands, but the basic foundations remain with updated adjustments or renovations. Even in times when the design may be completely abolished, the basic principles of construction remain, with new tools and design perhaps.

Likewise, considering another model, the McDonald's fast food chain provides a basic structural and procedural implementation plan for all of its locations. It does not matter if they are franchised or company owned. Quality control, staff training, standards for performance, mission and service delivery, customer service and satisfaction, and productivity and pricing remain constant across McDonald's branches.

In contrast, K–12 public education does not achieve success easily, because it does not have a consistent strategy that focuses on fundamentals that work and make for success. Consequently, there are disparate policies and systems that bring particular tensions that operate at cross-purposes. This creates unbalanced, unpredictable consequences and confusion. The problems are compounded when teachers are marginalized in an already complicated situation. Unlike private industry, keeping up with imposed, multifaceted changes causes educators to waste time and energy.

Principals and teachers do not have the luxury of time for analyzing and implementing answers to such questions as "What research-based school or instructional strategy can staff embrace and faithfully implement to consistently raise student achievement in classrooms and schools?" Private industry and business have research and development and marketing teams to constantly study this question in relation to products, sales, and outcomes. Then they proceed to implement, test, and manage with productivity, keeping profit margin in mind.

Fortune 500 companies such as General Electric encourage innovative, creative ideas by asking employees or focus groups, "What do you think works best, and what can we improve upon?" In business and industry, employees are trained to develop a well-thought-out strategy or systematically process a client through a sale. Strategies and language are taught to everyone for the purpose of delivering and implementing Plan A. If Plan A does not work, then employees are taught to use a specific Plan B. If the strategy is to make money, the employee is instructed and trained how best to make the sale.

History becomes the best predictor of what will help to meet the goal. Individuals are recruited and hired with the expectation that they have the knowledge and experience to perform the job, or they are willing to be trained and learn the mission and expectations for performance on the job. All that is left is guidance to learn the tools of the trade for consistent success.

Educators who have never worked in business where "time is money" are at a disadvantage when it comes to understanding the accomplishment of a mission and goals. The business sector does not commit to forces until there is a clear mission with a business plan. In like manner, school systems should not put students and teachers in harm's way by engaging in ever-changing juggling acts. Currently, the thinking goes something like this: "If it works, fine. If it doesn't, we'll try something else." There is no time to determine, "What should we do if the students do not learn what we indicated they would learn?"

An environment is not created for teachers to do their best work. Principals and teachers are steeped in dilemmas such as "Is the problem inappropriate, or are there too many gaps in a student's experiences and knowledge to access a viable solution?" Meanwhile, a student's valuable year is lost, reflected by declining test scores. Private industry usually has clear organizational structures and clearer lines and definitions of leadership roles and responsibilities. In education, little or divided power usually overrides educational goals for student achievement. There is a chasm between moneymaking organizations and those that deal in soft products like humans.

ALL IS NOT GOLDEN

Public education is a $600 billion enterprise that has caught the attention of entrepreneurial ventures and for-profit opportunists who have responded to the federal government's goals to create, innovate, and imagine how the billions of dollars could be spent. The business side of education has come front and center, and many of the billions of dollars that were intended for school and classroom improvement have been redirected by other forces that are taking public schools down a different path.

The problem is that business and industry are on life support as well, and all is not golden. There is a role for reform, transformation, and reinvention in the business sector also. There are massive layoffs, and small and large businesses closing in every direction. Long-standing stores are going out of business continually. There are economic downturns, plummeting revenue, and an unstable, fluctuating stock market. On the customer service side of the coin, serious improvement is needed. For instance, when automated prompts turn out to be the response when calling a business, sparks of ire surface as clients frantically try to reach a human to solve a problem or gain information.

Some corporations eliminate people who disagree with management or force people to leave if they do not fit in. Reform is needed in areas of flawed economic thinking that creates financial instability, questionable integrity, and corruption; corporate mergers that create economic havoc and unfair competition practices; and one-sided marketing principles. All of this transpires in the name of business, but the world of education and business are very different, and they operate in a different context. All is not well in the business model, and therefore to replicate its principles in education, for many, has the air of "buyer beware."

Education as a process sometimes has intangible outcomes. Private industry makes money or does not survive. In education, there is inertia, and some wonder how a teacher survives when students do not make their targets. It is important to understand that progress may have been made in many areas that were not tested. That is the quandary teachers face when defining and measuring the progress of students. In the process of education, educators must ask the deep, insightful questions that lead to investigating the deep principles and goals of educating all children. They must discuss the logic, the evidence, and the errors that have been made by educators and others. They must critically and creatively focus the goals ahead to bring students up to par for existence in the future world society.

Time is lost with people going back and forth on the relative merits of different models, strategies, plans, missions, goals, and solutions. The ultimate question is this: Did the students achieve the expected results? If not, why not? Are you satisfied with the results? If not, how will you make decisions to improve, alter, or eliminate what is being done? Researchers have been trying to figure out why schooling innovations have a long history of failure. They have concluded time and again that even with the best of intentions, new programs thrust upon people in their own workplace have little chance of survival (Sirotnik, 1985).

Larry Cuban (1988) has warned that school reformers frequently ignore the enabling conditions that are necessary for educators to lead, and therefore there has been "smothering" rather than "nourishing" of classroom, school, and district leadership and practices. He described school improvement efforts of the 1970s and 1980s as "reform by remote control." Although Cuban's comments referred to earlier decades, we could easily apply the thoughts to today. As emphasized earlier, classrooms and schools are reformed through calls for mandates, philanthropic and corporate plans, and theories by many in and outside education.

As much as most people believe that all students must be taught effectively in every school, accomplishing that task continues to be an elusive undertaking. As in other professions, such a strong focus on nonevidenced interpretations by anyone who thinks they have an evolutionary plan would wreak havoc and bring chaos to the integrity of the field. Such is the case in public education today. No one should be allowed to experiment with "other people's children" and their education, especially when they are learners who are the neediest and most dependent on a strong, equitable education as a way to progress.

As in other professions, order, coherence, and constancy of effort and purpose must be a part of the evolutionary process. Education as a field must remain professionalized. Educators must take a long, hard look at the conditions and outcomes of schools and strategically define and reinvent public education for these and future times. Order must be brought to the potential for chaos in the face of significant and ever-growing national, state, and local demands for revitalization. In the final determination, with proven, commonsense advances, it is a worthwhile and ongoing challenge.

Again, I turn to the commonsense philosophy of Ruth Herman Wells (2011), director of Youth Change Workshops:

> I wonder if any other industry is as prone to trends and fads as K–12 education. Every couple of years, a new model promises much, sweeps through the nation, then largely fades from view. Enter a new fad that promises much, and repeat. Endlessly. The trouble with most education models is that they're one-size-fits-all. In the real world, students come in all shapes and sizes, with all manner of challenges and barriers, and one simple approach will never fit all of them. To expect one basic model to fit all students coast to coast is like expecting one textbook to fit all students coast to coast.
>
> Instead of expecting a wide array of students to fit a model, maybe it's way past time to expect the model to fit the wide array of students. If there is to be consistency and collaboration in K–12 education, maybe it should coalesce around updated, common sense methods tailored and designed specifically to address the precise needs of that wide range of students. Maybe it's time to trade the trends for lasting, common sense teaching approaches that reach and teach all students.

CHAPTER 12

Meet the Kids

We must open the doors of opportunity. But we must also equip our people
to walk through those doors.

Lyndon B. Johnson

We have spent a great deal of time talking about struggling learners and
students who have difficulty in and out of school. We have talked about the
philosophy, theories, approaches, strategies, and responsibilities for addressing the needs of these students and youths. The time has come to meet some of
these students who flow through our nation's public schools. When one thinks
of youth in America today, many different things come to mind. I would like
to share a few examples:

1. The first image is Chuck, who is seventeen. He is not interested in school
   and is a top prospect for pro baseball. He says that he attends school
   because his dad wants him to graduate. Chuck's father cares about him,
   but does not know what to do to help. Chuck does come to school and is
   bright, but he is more interested in the social life. Chuck smokes mari-
   juana every day and has unprotected sex with many different partners.
   Chuck says that he does not know what he wants to do with his life. He
   does not have a job, but sells cocaine on the streets. Chuck carries a gun
   all the time because he has enemies who would like to see him dead.
   Recently Chuck was arrested and is awaiting a court date for a possible
   ten-year sentence for unlawful possession of a concealed weapon and
   possession of two ounces of cocaine in a school zone.
2. The next image is of Kim, who is twenty-five years old and has three
   children. All of the children have different fathers, but she is not really
   sure who they are. Kim dropped out of school in the tenth grade and has

never had a job. Her children are bright and enjoy school. At home, the children are constantly exposed to alcohol and witness domestic violence often. Kim's oldest child, Janet, is twelve and can already weigh drugs. Janet feels that it is not so bad having young children without a father; she uses her mother an as an example.

3. James is nineteen years old. He prefers to be called June Bug. He is about a year away from graduating from high school, and until two years ago, he was an honor student. He lives with both parents in a middle-class neighborhood. June Bug developed an interest in gangs and started hanging out with gang members daily. He thinks that it is cool and adds excitement to his life. James's parents pray each day that they will not get a call that their son has met with a fatal end.

4. Phyllis is thirty years old. Phyllis's parents are middle class, and she and her three siblings have had all the advantages afforded children in most affluent families. She graduated from high school with honors, but has delayed attending college until now. In the meantime, she spent the last years trying to "find herself," roaming from one job to another. She moved back to live with her parents recently, and she is now enrolled in a community college working toward a degree in teaching. After completing community college, she plans to transfer to a historically black college or university to earn a bachelor's degree, and then seek a job as a teacher.

5. Jamal is fifteen years old and lives at home with his mother and sister. Although he lives in a single-parent family, he has been provided for and supported in every way possible. Jamal attends high school daily and is a strong student. He is one of a few black students in his high school who takes Advanced Placement courses and has excellent grades. Jamal plays football, is involved in other extracurricular activities, and sings in the church choir. He has a girlfriend, Linda, who is a cheerleader and does well in school, too. Jamal has plans to go to college to become an engineer. His mother is very proud of him, and when he visits his father each week, he has a chance to talk to him about "boy/man"-type things. Jamal is well on his way to a productive future. His mother is well aware of the dangers in society faced by African American males and prays that he will stay on the right path and "trouble will not find him."

As illustrated in these scenarios, youths have a multitude of family conditions and life situations. At the dawn of the 1900s, a Swedish sociologist prophesied that the world was about to embark on a new era that would be known as the "century of the child." There was great faith that the progress of science would lead to a rebirth of human values and that the education of children would become the highest function of the nation.

Today, one would be unlikely to find a serious person who would describe the twenty-first century in those terms. Each scenario represents a breakdown in the process of child and youth development that can lead to possibilities or predicaments. This is why educators and others must untangle the web of ineffective schooling.

THE BEGINNING OF SHORTCOMINGS

A discussion about influences and education attainment has a great deal to do with acculturation and the sum of experiences, resources, and how time is spent. For example, as African Americans, why are there more skilled basketball players like Michael Jordan and Magic Johnson than tennis players like Arthur Ashe and Serena and Venus Williams? All clearly demonstrate intellectual and psychomotor gifts and other characteristics. Why are many African Americans not avid swimmers, even though they are "smart," motivated, and often interested? Why do many Americans not speak Spanish or another world language fluently, even when they have the motivation, interest, and resources to learn a new language?

All circumstances are matters of experiences, access to resources, and use of time. If any one component of development is missing in the socialization, acculturation, and schooling process, a gap or omission can occur. The above examples of playing basketball versus swimming or speaking English only versus a dual language illustrate the effects of where and how learning, practice, and mastery take place. This explains the differences in development, abilities, performance, and mastery in American classrooms today.

There are developmental differences, experiential differences within cultural groups, differences in languages and dialects spoken in the home, and differences in abilities and capabilities of people. These differences have little to do with intelligence, and more to do with experiences, resources, and ways people spend time on mastering different targets. All of these differences reflect the diversity, as opposed to the homogeneity, of American society. The results of all of these differences can be generalized to the context of public education.

Children come from rich background experiences that make the difference in their ability to achieve and excel with a high degree of confidence and performance in and out of school. This is especially true when background experiences and time spent are compatible with expectations of the educational environment and context. Background experiences can be taught and adjusted to help recover and reconstruct certain experiences, and dedicated time can be extended to advance learned and practical intelligence.

We are now talking about students who differ from the mainstream, who are able to adapt and renegotiate the context of school and their differing background and experiences. These are the low-income students and students of color who are able to spend adequate time and practice finding success in public schools. We have another set of students whose background experiences are far different from what is expected in the mainstream classroom and school. These are the students whose time is spent developing many gifts and talents that oftentimes are different from those valued in schools. In fact, often these students have expertise in street survival; applied mathematics used in street sales; mental math used to calculate grams, ounces, and kilos; or verbal debate skills through rhythmic rap or spoken-word readings and poetry. Some are children who have the gift of surviving life's tough conditions. Many mainstream students would not pass that test.

These are students who usually are identified as those who struggle to learn in school as we now structure them. Many of these students are the ones we read about in the statistics who are underperforming, underachieving, underserved, and acting out in our public schools today. They are students who most likely attend the many public schools across the nation.

Over the last two decades, we have been bombarded with negative data about underperforming students—African Americans in particular—who generally lag behind everyone in every area, including academic achievement. Cultural contingencies, differences in the way students are raised, differences in ways students are motivated to learn, differences in responses to the educational context, differences in family income and resources, and differences in society and support for the development of children have a great deal to do with the way various students are performing in school.

We know that the data can change with dedicated time, effort, and targeted resources that are used in commonsense ways. Many scholars and economists have presented data to document that, from the late 1960s to the 1980s, African American children in particular showed significant gains in educational attainment and achievement. In fact, achievement gaps of the past had begun to narrow and close. At that time, families and educators devoted a great deal of time and resources to developing balanced, successful school and life experiences for children.

A RECIPE FOR DEVELOPING POTENTIAL

Children must have support of school, family, society, educators, and community in three major areas—development of the mind, body, and heart:

1. *Intellectual development, or development of the mind:* Children must be exposed to the experiences, resources, and time to allow the intellect to stretch, grow, learn, compare, perceive, and reason. Teachers and families are responsible for development of the intellect through encouragement and the building of critical, sequential, functional skills in school and at home. The better the foundation (language, vocabulary, background knowledge, basic skills, concepts, good nutrition, parental care, stimulation and explanations for hands-on logic of the world that surrounds us), the better the chances for success in learning and life.

   Critical to the intellect, in American public schools, language is the determiner or basis for development of reading, comprehension, speaking, listening, and writing, which are crucial to positive school performance. The achievement/skills and learning gaps are not a mystery for most students who suffer from underperformance or struggle in school.

   When students lack cognitive knowledge and ability as expected in schools, when they are not developed intellectually as expected in school, and when they suffer from lack of security in a stable existence, the achievement gap begins at the earliest ages. It often persists during the process of schooling. In addition to the many children who come to school ready for the starting line, schools are faced with some who are already beyond the starting line and others who do not speak English or recognize the word *line*, and still others who do not know a line from a circle. These students often are far behind understanding what to do when a teacher says, "Ready, set, go!"

2. *Development of the body:* Related to the mind, a sound, healthy body stimulates the brain and allows a child to perform. Parents/guardians are responsible for providing nourishment and development of the body. Proper nutrition, physical activity and exercise, medical attention, a healthy attitude and lifestyle, positive social/emotional health, and a strong self-image are initially influenced by home life and environment. The healthy development of children is broadened by sensitive, caring teachers when children enter school.

   Support from families and educators is influenced by societal and political policies and decisions to provide adequate, equitable resources to assist and provide for needs, regardless of social and economic class. Communities also can influence healthy development through provision of recreational activities, facilities, and support geared toward families and children. There is no excuse for inadequate breakfast and lunch programs in schools, or hungry children, in this abundant country called America.

3. *Development of the heart:* Related to the mind and the physical being, the heart involves relationships, self-esteem, trust, kindness, consideration, spirit, values, emotion, and compassion. Development of these

qualities takes into consideration how a child comes to feel about self and others and gains self-confidence and ability as a person. An open, kind heart usually leads to an open mind. Parents and spiritual leaders are responsible for this development. If development of the heart is missing, children and youths lack social skills, behavior, attitudes, compassion, and responsibility to function within a group or in school, the community, or society.

Without concentrated development in all three areas, students will have shortcomings, no matter what their access and opportunity to learn. One area should not be developed at the expense of another. The result may be a child who does well in school, but uses an advanced book to hit another child over the head. Other possibilities include a timid, underdeveloped, emotionally weak child who cannot attend to lessons in school; a secure, bright child who is ill, resulting in numerous absences that create problems of keeping up in school; an athlete who cannot read; or children who cannot communicate socially, develop friendships, or manage their anger in a classroom or on the playground. These scenarios might provide reasons why many children have problems in school beyond the ability of most teachers to teach them.

In addition to those basic areas, children and youths must have a foundation that has different categories of knowledge, and they must stand ready to be assessed when called upon. If children have not engaged in and listened to complex language and have not been exposed to experiences where they know and learn when their thinking is flawed or inappropriate, they will use unsuitable language or create inappropriate situations. They will not know when to exhibit certain appropriate behaviors and when *not* to behave in certain ways in school, the community, or social settings.

Youths must know how to use the tools they have in the appropriate situation (cultural switching), so they can adjust to home, community, cultural, and school settings using appropriate language, behavior, and academic pursuits. This would eliminate certain inappropriate behaviors in school, such as bending to peer pressure to not perform to the highest academic levels or to move away from values, and not understanding how to switch to appropriate work and school behavior versus street or community stances as acceptable group standards in public or on the job.

The adults in the lives of children must help eliminate omissions in experiences and knowledge. They must provide experiences for developing flexibility in the use of language, thinking, empathy, and compassion. Children must have opportunities to model, practice, and reinforce behaviors that are expected in society, school, and the work environment. Schools must take responsibility for helping students learn, understand, and extend experiences and knowledge. The community and society must provide adequate access to resources and hold families and educators responsible for appropriate use of those resources.

Certainly we cannot afford to continue to lose generations of students throughout the twenty-first century. We are now at a time and state that we can move to the future by improving upon the interlocking issues that affect the outcomes of public education. The direction we decide take to improve circumstances for youths and young adults like Chuck, Kim, James/June Bug, Phyllis, Jamal, and many others represents the future,

We need to think deeply about how our schools and children in need got to where they are today and, at the same time, address some of the pain points as educators. Many of the mediating factors that facilitate and influence performance and academic achievement can be bolstered. And some of the major internal and external factors that might be causing stagnation and discontinuity for children and their school achievement can be removed. Many learning problems and conditions of school failure are not a mystery, nor do they require throwing ideas into the air to see which one will not boomerang. There are logical answers for logical conditions.

If our public schools are to produce citizens ready to meet the challenges of today's world, we need to look at how each child is learning and take into account the nonschool factors that affect how children learn. We cannot succeed with all children without focusing on the individual needs of each child. Public education is stronger when the public is on board. Its success depends on the commitment of the entire community, working in partnership to ensure that *each child is ready for school, the school is ready for all children*, and *every student learns to her or his potential.*

FINAL THOUGHTS

If there are uncertainties about Response to Intervention, it is because RtI lacks history, clarity, or a roadmap to "build the ship while driving and navigating it." Like the *Titanic*, there is no precise knowledge of how to avoid the icebergs, difficult waters, buoys, and obstinate obstacles. Also, there is no certainty that one will reach the next port of call or final destination. This is true of most new school reform initiatives or innovative practices in public education today.

Educators are working against a complicated mix of challenges and barriers to proficient learning. Reforming and providing inclusive educational practices is part of the mission that educators must continue to struggle with on behalf of all students. Understanding teaching, learning, identifying, and knowing how to teach and provide accurate interventions are key parts of the responsibility. Knowing how to assess, recognize, and intervene in learning failure early and to implement appropriate organizational and program structures is an additional requirement. Most important, learning to streamline, personalize, and employ the most effective resources and corrective processes systemically will continue to be a serious mission for teachers and related others.

RtI must avoid becoming another convoluted, quick-fix school solution that does not recognize the complexities of general and special education. It is an example of an innovation that can become a victim, like many of the past classroom improvement strategies that are now on the list of unsuccessful innovative efforts to improve public schooling. Whenever we address the needs of students in public and education policy, we are talking about a very diverse, intricate set of student and teacher needs. We are also highlighting a blend of in-school and out-of-school dynamics that must be strategically approached on behalf of individual children and families.

Most important, through conversations and debate, educator professional development, research, reflection, and evaluation, all stakeholders must look more deeply into what might be causing struggles and school failure beyond the seemingly obvious reasons. This is critical to the equity agenda, especially for students who have been disproportionately affected.

As a concluding point, part of the optimum mix for providing equity in student learning includes developing and valuing the talent, skills, and people needed to deliver the necessary improvements. This means eliminating the rhetoric and issues that may be preventing or discouraging the ability of teachers to do their work.

For all educators, bringing together the right combination of essential ingredients for each child's situation involves having the capability to identify which elements provide the most comprehensive understanding of what students need to learn effectively and efficiently. Biancarosa and Snow (2004, p. 12) provided the most insightful prescription for the potential of a long-term impact of Response to Intervention:

> In the medical profession, treatment needs to be tailored to an individual patient's needs; at times, more than one intervention is needed to effectively treat a patient. Similarly, educators need to test mixes of intervention elements to find the ones that work best for students with different needs.

Appendix: A Comprehensive Curriculum/RtI Design Tool

A Framework for Designing and Linking Systemic Curriculum, Instruction, Assessment, and Response to Intervention

I. COMPREHENSIVE CURRICULUM DESIGN GUIDELINES
   A. Review and prioritize common essential learning standards in and across disciplines.
   B. Define curriculum areas of interest.
   C. Identify areas of continuity and connections between team members and groups.
   D. Develop long-term goals and missions for curriculum guidelines matched to common core or state/local learning standards and assessment data.

II. NEEDS ASSESSMENT
   A. Analyze data based on an identified district or school needs assessment, standardized test data, and/or appropriate universal screening data.
   B. Refine areas of interests from broad to specific (e.g., reading, analytical skills, comprehension, number sense, etc.).
   C. Categorize identified needs and weaknesses particular to students' age, stage, grade, and/or performance level.
   D. *Knowledge/skills obtained*
      1. Based on universal and state assessments, generally list skills that students do well in the school, district, or within a grade level.
      2. Initially analyze total district or school outcomes to broaden awareness of what students already know across the grade and school levels.
   E. *Knowledge/skills needed*
      1. Generally list all skills that students need for specific development and continuity (i.e., by school, class, or individual).
   F. Analyze existing preK–12 curriculum objectives for repetitions, if available.
      1. Using a graphic organizer or web, examine repetitions according to themes concepts, or skills.

123

2. Decide which can be consolidated and eliminated. This can be done with an interactive whiteboard, laptop and projector, or long butcher paper and markers.

3. Color-code and enlarge objectives for viewing and analyzing for redundancy across various grade levels and disciplines (subject matter). This can be done on an interactive whiteboard or with marking pens.

G. Categorize items on the lists into curriculum subject areas.

1. Look for commonalities to eliminate the number of needs across the curriculum; for example, note common related skills, concepts, and universal themes.

H. Redefine curriculum areas based on categorization and the needs assessment data.

I. Prioritize one list of general education curriculum areas that are noted as "weak skills" areas using three categories of importance and mastery:

1. *Essential*
   a. Crucial, nonnegotiable content knowledge, skills, and abilities.
   b. Essential skills and knowledge are high in structure and importance. They are the most critical or basic knowledge and skills needed for understanding and applying a discipline.
   c. Learning standards, skills, and knowledge that must be taught to all students at various levels of difficulty and complexity.

2. *Important*
   a. Critical but not essential skills, abilities, and knowledge. Add depth to content.
   b. Goes beyond to add depth to essential knowledge to broaden and ensure understanding.
   c. For example, because teachers know that students have difficulty learning fractions, they might decide to teach another level of understanding to increase the importance through an applied or real-life activity.

3. *"Nice to do"*
   a. Not critical or necessarily connected or related to essential or important knowledge, information, or related skill attainment.
   b. The spontaneous, planned, unplanned, or unconnected lessons and activities that one may enjoy teaching, but do not connect to essential to important skills in the intended curriculum.

J. Prioritize a second list for advanced students, indicating curriculum areas still in need of development, if that is the focus for curriculum development.

K. List the skills prioritized in the "essential" category under the correct general and advanced curriculum area(s).

L. Organize and categorize under broad concepts if desired, and prioritize similar essential skills in interdisciplinary groups, if appropriate (i.e., English/language arts, social studies/history, health and physical education).

III. COMPARATIVE CURRICULUM OFFERINGS—MANAGEABILITY AND CONTENT FOR ALL

   A. In team groupings, first within a discipline, then in multidisciplinary teams, use a district curriculum guide for a particular grade level, course, or stage of development.

      1. List the standard information or learning standards that all students in each category should know (i.e., grade 3, geometry, nongraded, grade 11, etc.).

      2. From the above, as a team, compare, eliminate unnecessary curriculum concepts or skills, and add others that are missing that will assist in the essential development of students.

   B. Provide copies of each team's articulated curriculum draft to each team so it can be compared.

      1. Assess for manageability, continuity, flexibility, relevancy, repetition, relevancy, content integrity, and coherence.

      2. Monitor between teams and watch for excessive redundancy and lack of continuity for skills introduced, reinforced, and mastered.

      3. Collaboratively work between teams or team chairpersons. Finalize the curriculum articulation across grades, prekindergarten to grade 12.

      4. Ensure that diverse perspectives and multicultural content are integrally interwoven into the curriculum content.

IV. OBJECTIVES

   A. Develop specific performance objectives for each curriculum area that are linked to the prioritized core learning standards.

      1. Develop skills-continuum-based needs assessment data and each team's agreed-upon articulated curriculum guidelines or framework that was developed in Step III.

      2. Each team should develop the draft of the articulated curriculum into "big ideas," broad concepts, and universal themes, starting from expected outcomes in grades 12 to kindergarten, if desired.

      3. Collaborate between teams or with team chairpersons to determine interrelated themes and concepts across disciplines. Organize in a developmentally appropriate sequence or continuum.

      4. Based on learning standards and common curriculum, special-needs team members should define extended objectives and activities that can provide access to all students. This will serve as the basis for selection of strategies for below-level and advanced students who need Tier 1 and/or 2 interventions.

V. IMPLEMENTATION
  A. Identify or develop instructional and program strategies.
    1. Brainstorm strategies for instruction (e.g., personalized, team teaching, peer teaching, interest groups, direct instruction, self-contained, inclusion, departmentalized, interdisciplinary, mixed groupings, etc.).
    2. Consider varying modes of instruction at different levels of depth, breadth, and complexity for different students.
    3. Consider the varying levels of teacher and student skills and experiences in selecting strategies.
    4. Determine the appropriateness of strategies reflecting ongoing student data on academic strengths and weaknesses and effectiveness of instruction.
  B. Brainstorm and identify evidence-based instruction models.
    1. Identify strategies noted for closing content gaps and omissions in the curriculum.
    2. Brainstorm interventions, acceleration techniques, and lesson ideas for various grade and school levels.
    3. Include time frames or pacing, formative assessment techniques, roles and areas of responsibility, resources, and accommodations for RtI multitiered levels.
    4. Include an RtI Design Team for researching and identifying models for multitiered frameworks that seem appropriate for Tier 1, Tier 2, and Tier 3 intensities. This will be the first working draft for each curriculum area.
    5. The Response Design Team and Curriculum Design Team collaborate on placing potential interventions into tiers to address specific weak skills as a working draft.
    6. The Response Design Team researches and identifies enabling evidenced interventions, assessment tools, and strategies that address emotional/social, behavior, attendance, and other factors.
      a. Identify in-school interventions first, then identify out-of-school interventions.
      b. Identify their cost, usefulness, and intended targeted skills and assessments.
  C. Compare identified strategies and resources as appropriate for specific targeted populations.
    1. Include tier levels for special education, gifted and talented, literacy and mathematics underachievers, English-language learners, below-level readers, off-track students, overage students, and so forth.
  D. Determine modes and methods of instruction that could be utilized by the team. Examples include the following:
    1. Large-/Small-Group/Direct Instruction

2. Personalized, Self-paced, Self-Directed

3. Peer Teaching/Support Teams/Coteaching/Inclusion

4. Student-Centered Learning/Facilitation

5. Flexible Skills Group/Mixed Ability/Independent Learning

6. Simulated (Service, Simulations, Role Plays, Internships, Coaching, Video Diaries, Portfolios, etc.)

7. Negotiated Learning/Contracts/Learning Communities

8. Critical Theory/Seminars/Socratic Method of Inquiry (articulate an idea and fully discuss all elements in various settings)

9. Project-based/Problem-based/Experiential Learning

10. Virtual/Distance Learning/Online Tutorials/Computer-Assisted Learning

11. Prevention, Intervention/Acceleration/Advanced Learning

12. Lecture, Laboratory, Discussion

E. Response Design Team researches, identifies, and determines extension or alternative methods for each instructional mode that allows similar experiences at different levels of involvement, abilities, skills, and complexity.

1. Include potential extended/alternative methods of multitiered interventions in the RtI draft framework.

2. Identify educational options that will accelerate or extend learning and maximize success for every child inside and outside the general classrooms (i.e., adjustments in school curriculum and placement, cross-grade grouping, multi-grade classrooms, advanced courses/honors preparation and course offerings that respond to a variety of high-potential and high-ability students, virtual learning courses, college readiness programs designed to accelerate learning for middle and high school students who show gifted potential, and dual high school/college courses/entry).

3. Decide on the role of staff members needed, and define the particular mode of instruction that each member will be responsible for researching and developing in each curriculum content area.

F. Determine a menu of instructional and learning tools that can support teaching and learning.

1. Audio/Visual/Interactive and Multimedia

2. Network-based and Computer-Mediated/Internet Resources

3. Interactive Whiteboards/Laptop Computers/iPods/iPads, etc.

4. Print Materials/Products and Digital/Electronic Displays

5. E-mail/Text Messaging, etc.

6. Web Pages/Newsgroups/Storyboards

7. Video Conferencing/Skyping

8. Textbooks (Print)/Supplemental Materials/Electronic Textbooks

9. Presentation Software/Authoring Systems

G. Response Design Team researches, identifies, and determines re-searched alternative learning and instructional tools and resources that allow similar experiences at different levels of involvement, skills, abilities, and complexity.

H. Develop an organizational plan for the use of the facility or classroom. For example:

1. Instructional Areas/Learning Centers/Student Seating
2. Technology Use/Storage/Internet Access
3. Teaching and Learning Styles
4. Instructional/Independent Activities/Before- or After-School/ Enrichment Programs
5. Research/Media/Materials/Resources
6. Instructional Assistants/Volunteers/Intervention Specialists
7. Inclusion/Interventions/Differentiated Lessons
8. Scheduling/Routines/Classroom Management Procedures
9. Preparation/Released Time/Planning Areas
10. Assessment/ Progress Monitoring, Screening Tools

I. Assemble an Interdisciplinary Response Design Team to refine the RtI framework.

1. Members should include thirteen to fifteen people, consisting of special education teachers, related service providers, and reading, math, and other content specialists.
2. Include a representative from assessment, student services, a be-havior specialist, counseling and guidance, special programs, gifted education, health workers, an out-of-school agency representative, and so forth.
3. Their role will be to research, identify, and determine what accom-modations and modifications are needed for similar experiences at different levels of skills, abilities, and complexity.

VI. RESPONSE TO INTERVENTION (RtI) FRAMEWORK DEVELOP-MENT

A. Collaborate and define roles for organizational responsibilities and timelines for each member, including support staff such as speech pathologists, behavior specialists, and psychologists.

B. Determine in- and out-of-school social/health workers, counselors, mentors, instructional assistants, and others who might be involved in the delivery of intervention techniques.

C. Collaborate and complete schedules for academic and operational plans (e.g., lunch, recess, supplemental programs, RtI tiers, schedules, team meetings, planning, staff data analysis days, course schedules, etc.).

D. Explore and decide on an RtI framework model and strategies for development of a comprehensive framework prototype for tier levels.

1. Identify and verify evidence-based interventions and resources for elementary, middle, and high schools involving attendance, behavior, and proficiency needs in literacy and mathematics.

E. Develop Tier 1 (Universal), Tier 2 (Targeted), and Tier 3 (Intensive) frameworks for how to meet the unmet needs of struggling, advanced, and off-track learners.

F. Involve assessment and evaluation staff in the research and identification of appropriate assessments (formative, diagnostic, and standardized) for evaluating progress of core curriculum for varied learners.

1. Involve assessment and evaluation staff to research, identify, and select appropriate assessments for academic, behavior, and psychosocial behaviors, gifted education, and other special needs.

G. Collaborate with the General Education Curriculum Design Team to research and explore options for effective interventions, assessment, procedures, processes, and models of best practice for literacy and other content area needs.

1. Explore and identify in- and out-of-school challenges and resources that undermine academic success in each content area and across the curriculum.

2. Identify existing and new evidenced or promising interventions and acceleration strategies that are recommended to ensure that students are engaged in the learning process.

3. Address the range of students' needs during curriculum implementation and within the tier levels of a RtI framework.

4. Explore interventions and assessments that improve, track, and measure attendance, truancy, safety, and so forth.

5. Involve district technology information management staff in these decisions.

H. Identify materials and resources that feature student-centered pedagogy, and support and broaden the understanding of how to increase levels of difficulty and rigor, including appropriate hardware, software, and digital tools matched to instruction and interventions.

1. Match developmental considerations for students in terms of skill levels, interests, and abilities.

2. Identify appropriate administrative tools needed for assessment, tracking, monitoring, and recordkeeping.

3. Determine what current staff and funding and additional funding, resource support, and staff may be needed to support curriculum and RtI implementation.

I. Brainstorm the role of parents, out-of-school providers, and family for academic, social/emotional, and behavior engagement and support.

J. Research past successful practices as well as existing, current, and new methods and programs, evaluations, requirements, costs, purposes, strategies, and so forth.

VII. IMPLEMENTATION PLAN

   A. Recommend a comprehensive action plan for inclusion of in- and out-of-school-related provisions to support students with and without academic and behavior disabilities.

      1. Involve the special education staff and specific other general education and support staff in this process as necessary.

      2. Collaboratively recommend an RtI district-wide framework, including protocols, procedures, resources, contingencies, timelines, interventions, implementation, staff training, and so on for local school consideration.

      3. Include school principals at each school level and other appropriate staff in the recommendation of the framework.

         a. Ensure the Response to Intervention Draft Framework includes all best-practice components that support effective implementation of the District-wide Comprehensive Curriculum Framework as the first step in Tier 1.

         b. Ensure strong evaluation of effectiveness of teaching and fidelity of instruction and interventions in the general classroom in terms of the intended curriculum, instructional strategies, resources, assessments, and evaluation of intervention tier responses before moving students to more intense tiers.

   B. Develop and include a recommended staff development plan that will not overlap with comprehensive curriculum design implementation (see Step X below).

      1. Scaffold the professional development implementation plan by regions, school or grade levels, core subjects or departments, and so forth.

      2. This should be done in concert with the curriculum planning process.

      3. Determine follow-up and embedded approaches and support in the classroom, such as coaches, helping teachers, mentors, trainer of trainers, and so on.

   C. Involve the director of curriculum and instruction, professional development, instructional technology, special programs, special education, gifted education, and English-language learners (ELL) in the process.

VIII. EVALUATION SYSTEM

    A. Develop or identify a universal screening tool, evaluative bench-marks, and measures for student gains and outcomes. Match them to curriculum priorities and RtI goals and objectives.

    B. Evaluate assessment and data tools for user-friendliness, manage-ability, and alignment with curriculum and performance data for individual students. Assessments needed:

        1. *Universal screening:* Assessments and diagnostic tools to deter-mine proficiencies in specific content or skill areas for individual and group needs.

        2. *Quantitative tests:* A district or school standardized test that mea-sures student academic growth over the course of a school year.

        3. *Provision for comparative data of individual, class, school, dis-trict, and cohort student performance over time, usually admin-istered by the classroom teacher or others, generally at the end of a school year.*

        4. *Qualitative assessments:* Formal and informal assessments, such as teacher comments; survey data; or grade- or skills-specific, subject-area, or diagnostic tests, questionnaires, behavior, or so-cial/emotional inventories or tools.

            a. Data can be provided by teachers, parents, students, support staff, and others who can offer additional information on aca-demic efforts and other contingencies, such as behavior and social-emotional variables, and so on.

            b. *Diagnostic formative assessments:* Quick informal checks on skills development or monitoring of progress, usually tracked over four- to eight-week intervals to determine if academic growth is occurring at the expected rate.

            c. *Teacher-made tools* and others focused on individual learning styles, ability, skills, readiness, or knowledge attainment, and so forth.

            d. A *pre- and posttest feature* for end-of-course, skills or content or curriculum attainment, and so on, to monitor growth and progress in comparison to learning standards or the need to adjust materials, instruction, or level of intensity.

    C. Identify tools for gifted education referral, identification, and place-ment.

    D. Align special education, ELL, prekindergarten, and other screening identification and referral processes and procedures.

E. Plan a process to test assessment tools and identification processes for cultural, language, and gender bias and other contingencies.

F. Identify a process, tool, or Web-based system for data gathering, analysis, and recordkeeping compatible with the district's and school's student information management system. Analyze a learning management system for compatibility and user friendliness, cost-effectiveness, and utility.

G. Assess overall classroom, school, and district achievement data in selected priority curriculum areas.

H. Provide a strategy such as "data days" during staff/planning meeting for review of student progress and discussions about data across levels and content areas, at least once monthly.

IX. COVERAGE AND MANAGEABILITY OF THE OVERFULL CURRICULUM

A. After completion of development of two or three core curriculum areas as a priority, additional areas can be selected, developed, and scheduled for completion by the team as noted above. Areas to be considered:

1. Additional core areas if all have not been covered initially. For example, if the team selected English/language arts, mathematics, and science, then social studies/history should be selected along with a related career/technical education area at this point.

2. Intervention programs related to core curriculum and matched to student needs should be aligned, including special education, ELL, overage, dropout recovery, reading, speech, and language programs; mathematics acceleration; gifted and talented; and so on.

3. Accommodations and modifications for acceleration and advancement should be aligned and broadened to meet curriculum requirements.

4. Other content areas that are compatible and related to the core and common standards should be selected.

B. Elective courses should be developed in like manner.

1. Career/Technical Education
2. World Languages
3. Art
4. Music
5. Health/Physical Education, etc. Note: Health/physical education could be selected along with science to focus on interrelated concepts or subject area content.

C. Transfer and applied learning

1. Career/vocational/technical courses, themes, common standards, and applied learning could be developed simultaneously to provide transfer of knowledge to real life and/or workplace experiences.

2. Suggested experiential learning should be embedded in the curriculum, such as the following:
   a. Aligned and related field trips across various grade and school levels matched to curriculum and learning standard priorities.
   b. Field trips and related out-of-school experiences that provide background knowledge for essential concepts.
   c. Internships, externships, apprenticeships, dual enrollment, job shadowing, work training, and exchange programs matched to essential skills and course requirements for certification, advanced learning, project-based learning, independent study and research, and so forth.

D. Supplemental programs should be aligned, including out-of-school partnerships and services, and sources should be linked to essential curriculum and classroom expectations, including public and private prekindergarten providers as a prevention strategy.
   1. Identify, evaluate, and prioritize which strategies and programs are evidence based and cost-effective and have long-term outcomes that improve and enhance student learning and achievement.
      a. Eliminate those that are merely "nice to do" or "important."
      b. Maintain essential, proven strategies and programs that have evidence of impact and return on investment for prevention, intervention, or support of academic or behavior student growth.
      c. This exercise will assist in determining which strategies, programs, and resources are most useful for making decisions on priorities for interventions and expenditures for supplemental resources and programs.
   2. Align volunteers and evaluate and align community/business partnership providers based on previous steps.

E. Develop a total school schedule for implementation of the entire curriculum. Organize full-day, weekly, blocked, or monthly implementation.

F. Review curriculum implementation on a monthly, quarterly, or semester basis. A needs assessment will be necessary periodically to determine the relevancy of the curriculum in terms of student needs and interests and the changing priorities and practices in teaching, learning, content knowledge, or skills development.

X. TEAM/STAFF DEVELOPMENT

A. Staff/professional development for effective implementation: Review the plan in Step VII, Part B.

B. Needs assessment
   1. Identify or develop a needs assessment for staff in-service to assist with understanding the curriculum design, related data analysis, and instructional decision-making needed. Suggestions include:

      a. Determining appropriate lessons
      b. Determining and implementing strategies with fidelity
      c. Determining and delivering prevention/intervention techniques
      d. Diagnosing and assessing effective learning
      e. Student assessments, identified instructional
      f. Linking instructional strategies and resources
      g. Learning dimensions matched to curriculum priorities and objectives
      h. Cultural and learning contingencies
      i. Determining what professional development strategies are needed to develop teacher capacity and continual improvement
      j. Identifying and implementing student supports to gain access to instruction

C. Program priorities
    1. Identify no more than five program or instructional priorities or goals per year for the focus of professional development.
    2. Reduce the number, depending on the strength of the overall staff.

D. Response to Intervention (RtI)
    1. Consider RtI as a second level of new paradigm requiring extensive staff development at various levels of understanding and implementation.
    2. Teachers who are ready for advanced levels of professional development of curriculum implementation are the most prepared to begin staff training for RtI processes and implementation.
      a. The goals for professional development should remain constant as a strategic priority for three to five years or more.
      b. Considerations must be made for:
        1. school and classroom-level plan
        2. data gathering for barriers and challenges
        3. curriculum modifications and adjustments
        4. course implementation and identification
        5. implementation of interventions at each grade and school level
    3. Outline role changes for general classroom teachers, especially at the secondary level.
    4. Note changing responsibilities for support staff and provide assistance with those changes.
    5. Research and match in- and out-of-school providers/partners with needs.
    6. Coordinate special education (academic, social/emotional, behavior) and ELL needs, including family connections for student growth and development.

7. Include staff needed for mastery of technological tools and resources associated with recordkeeping, management of RtI processes and procedures, data collection, and teaching and learning.

E. Cultural contingencies/background knowledge

1. Investigate how to include various cultural activities, strategies, content, knowledge, information, examples, resources (including human), and background information to ensure content relevance for all varied learners.

F. Classroom and behavior management

1. Determine techniques and programs that address how to engage students in the curriculum and RtI processes so as not to stigmatize them, but rather provide a sense of support, acceleration, and participation.

2. Explore and identify evidence-based assessments and programs that strengthen universal school and classroom management abilities and improve student behavior in the three RtI tiers.

3. Include community resources and support, as well as social workers, counselors, a psychologist, and so forth.

G. In- and out-of-school linkages (whole child, whole village)

1. Determine the role of parents, out-of-school providers, family, and community in assisting with curriculum and RtI implementation (e.g., homework, transition, graduation and course-taking progression, mentors, volunteers, city agencies, tutors, etc.).

2. Consider academic, social/emotional, and behavior support needed for classroom participation and achievement. Align within the design of RtI guidelines and procedures.

H. English-language learners

1. Curriculum components and resources may need to be provided in various languages reflective of staff and students (i.e., print and nonprint media, classroom-learning resources).

2. Core materials may need to be translated into Spanish, for example, to accommodate students whose predominant language is not English.

I. Early learning

1. Determine role of prekindergarten/kindergarten alignment matched to developmentally appropriate curriculum expectations.

2. Develop an articulation strategy for public/private preschool providers and kindergarten teachers, especially in underperforming schools (i.e., curriculum information exchange meetings, kindergarten curriculum orientation and planning sessions, community/parent kindergarten visitation/information curriculum information

meeting to explain expectations prior to the beginning of the school year, etc.).

J. Proposals for future staff development

1. One or two additional areas of training can be planned for future focus and curriculum implementation and tier advancement, for example, in addition to the three curriculum and instructional priorities outlined earlier.

2. Staff development should be designed around the following topics and notions:

    a. Curriculum mapping, curriculum development, and instructional planning in and among disciplines, grades, and school levels.

    b. Technology: The consensus of the team might be to implement a new student/information or learning management system, instructional materials, hardware and software, or an RtI management system.

    c. Integrating technologies and digital sources and tools into instructional planning and strategies in grade- and content-level meetings, peer coaching, team teaching, and support over time.

    d. Response to Intervention team planning, data analysis, tier-level development, progress monitoring, assessment and analysis, and evaluation of student data and other techniques.

    e. Staff evaluation of evidenced intervention strategies, programs, tools, and out-of-school factors and resources.

    f. Special and general education teachers' team planning and meetings, team and coteaching, embedded support and planning, curriculum modifications and accommodations, and so on.

    g. Special education, gifted education, alternative learners, students of color, and ELL as dimensions of learning.

    h. Focused staff development support, embedded coaching in the classroom, grade-level or content-level meetings over time, and follow-through to ensure success of the entire curriculum and RtI framework design.

    i. Staff development activities must be continuous and each staff person must make a commitment to development until mastery.

    j. School leadership development to maintain the focus of established priorities, providing the resources and support needed for success and navigating change in education.

    k. Mentors, coaches, peers, and collegial team development to assist with training new staff, substitutes, or others who need

assistance with the implementation of the curriculum and RtI frameworks.

l. School department leaders and supervisors should participate in professional development strands, as well as provide mechanisms for practice among and between teachers, grades, and school levels to bring implementation to scale.

m. Factors that influence student learning customized to the local staff and student population.

n. Coaches and helping teachers training to assist with peer feedback, assessing fidelity of implementation and interventions, and implementation of the curriculum.

XI. CELEBRATION/INCENTIVES

A. When curriculum goals have been met and maintained, as reflected by student performance and achievement outcomes in classrooms, and when assessments, teaching and learning tools, and resources are implemented effectively by at least 80 percent of the staff, a celebration should be planned to acknowledge team effort and success.

B. Staff and student accomplishments should be reflected, documented, and marketed through visible public relations mechanisms throughout the school and community.

C. Brainstorm desirable, feasible incentives. As teachers demonstrate effort, peers and school leaders should provide growth and improvement models of praise and encouragement. Keep it simple. (Teachers often value the gift of time in addition to monetary incentives.)

D. As individuals and groups of students show effort and advancement through progress monitoring, assessments, daily lessons, or other indicators:

1. Teachers should provide positive reinforcement and acknowledgment.

2. Brainstorm, research, and identify various techniques for celebrations, encouragement, acknowledgment, and rewards for both adults (i.e., staff and parents) and students.

E. As individual and groups of students show effort and progress in behavior and attendance, individually or in group learning experiences and academic plans, positive reinforcement and acknowledgment should be readily provided by principals, teachers, and related staff.

F. As individual students show effort and progress in any way that warrants recognition, teachers and leaders should inform parents/guardians and out-of-school providers through a positive phone call, e-mail, text, or other visible ways that can be brainstormed and shared.

1. This will encourage positive parent/family engagement and support of school efforts.
2. It will link the impact of in- and out-of-school efforts, develop support for student gains and outcomes, and reinforce responsible citizenship and self-management.

References

Anderson, C. W. 1989. The role of education in the academic disciplines in teacher education. In *Research perspectives on the graduate preparation of teachers*, ed. A. Woolfolk, 88–107. Englewood Cliffs, NJ: Prentice Hall.

Artiles, A. J. 2007. Challenges to RtI models: Equity and cultural considerations [PowerPoint presentation]. National Center for Culturally Responsive Education Systems. Available at http://www.rti4success.org/pdf/rti-cop_9-07.pdf.

Berry, B., M. Hoke, and E. Hirsch. 2004. The search for highly qualified teachers [electronic version]. *Phi Delta Kappan* 85 (9): 684–89.

Biancarosa, G., and C. E. Snow. 2004. *Reading next: A vision for action and research in middle and high school literacy.* Washington, DC: Alliance for Excellent Education.

Billingsly, W. 2009. Response to Intervention: Seattle Public Schools. Presentation made at the Washington Alliance of Black School Educators, March, Seattle.

Borg, L. 2010. Providence's Bailey Elementary School combines education, community outreach. *Providence Journal*, July 7.

Boykin, W. L. 2010. About the takeover of DCPS and other urban districts [blog]. Retrieved on October 12, 2010, from http://groups.yahoo.com/group/EN4abse/.

Burns, M. K., and J. E. Ysseldyke. 2006. Comparison of existing Response-to-Intervention models to identify and answer implementation questions. *Communiqué* 34 (5). Available at http://www.nasponline.org/publications/cq/cq345rti_burns.aspx.

Cuban, L. 1988. *The managerial imperative and the practices of leadership in schools.* Albany: State University of New York Press.

Dougherty, C. 2010. Using the right data to determine if high school interventions are working to prepare students for college and careers. National High School Center at the American Institutes for Research. Retrieved on May 4, 2010, from http://groups.yahoo.com/group/EN4abse/.

Edmonds, R. R. 1982. Programs of school improvement: An overview. Paper presented at the National Invitational Conference, "Research on Teaching: Implications for Practice," February 25–27, 1982, Warrenton, Virginia. Retrieved from www.erc.ed.gov:80/PDFS/ED221536.pdf.

Editorial Projects in Education Research Center. 2011. National graduation rate rebounds: 1.2 million students still fail to earn diplomas. Press release, June 7. Available at http://www.edweek.org/media/diplomascount2011_pressrelease.pdf.

Forys, K. A. 1989. Alternatives for drop-outs. *Curriculum in Context* 21 (2): 26–27.

Goldstein, L. 1999. The relational zone: The role of caring relationships in the co-construction of mind. *American Educational Research Journal* 36 (3): 647–73.

Homer, R. H., G. Sugai, K. Smolkowski, L. Eber, J. Nakasoto, A. W. Todd, and J. Esperanza. 2009. Randomized, wait-listed controlled effectiveness trial assessing school-wide positive behavior support in elementary schools. *Journal of Positive Behavior Interventions* 11 (3): 133–44. Available at http://pbi.sagepub.com/cgi/content/abstract/11/3/133.

Hunter, J. E., and F. L. Schmidt. 1996. Cumulative research knowledge and social policy formulation: The critical role of meta-analysis. *Psychology, Public Policy, and Law* 2 (2): 324–47. Retrieved from http://conium.org/~maccoun/PP279_Hunter.pdf.

Jackson, P. L. 2010. The war between black children and the world in which they live. *EdNews You Can Use*. Special on the "GAP," 1, 2. Retrieved on August 28, 2010, from www.blackstar1000ameritech.net.

Lewis, C., D. Garrison-Wade, M. Scott, B. Douglas, and V. Middleton. 2004. A synthesis of evidence-based research on the status of African American teachers 50 years after Brown and its impact on African American student achievement: Implications for teachers and administrators. *Journal of Teaching and Learning in Diverse Settings* 2 (1): 99–124. Retrieved from http://www.piteburglive.com/xpittsburgtribu/news/pittsburgh/print_9=690415.html.

Livingston, J. N., and C. Nahimana. 2006. Problem child or problem context? An ecological approach to young black males. *Reclaiming Children and Youth* 14 (4): 209–14.

Los Angeles Unified School District. 2011. CBITS. http://www.tsaforschools.org/index.php?option=com_content&task=view&id=81&Itemid=69.

Marshall, J. 2007–2008. Return on learning (ROL) is the new ROI. [SIIA] *Upgrade* (December–January): 28–30. Retrieved from www.spectrumk12.com/news/in_the_news/.

National Alliance of Black School Educators and Council of Exceptional Children. 2002. *Addressing over-representation of African American students in special education: The pre-referral intervention process: An administrator's guide.* Washington, DC: Special Education Programs.

National High School Center, National Center on Response to Intervention, and Center on Instruction. 2010. *Tiered interventions in high schools: Using preliminary "lessons learned" to guide ongoing discussion.* Washington, DC: American Institutes for Research. Available at www.betterhighschools.org/pubs/documents/HSTII_LessonsLearned.pdf.

National Joint Committee on Learning Disabilities. 2005. *Responsiveness to intervention and learning disabilities.* Washington, DC: National Joint Committee on Learning Disabilities.

Newmann, F., B. King, and P. Youngs. 2000. Lessons from urban elementary schools. *American Journal of Education* 108 (4): 259–99.

Ortiz, S. 2001. Assessment of cognitive abilities in Hispanic children. *Seminars in Speech and Language* 22 (1): 17–27.

Parsad, B., L. Lewis, and E. Farris. 2001. Teacher preparation and professional development, 2000. NCES 2001-008. Washington, DC: U.S. Department of Education, National Center for Education Statistics.

Pierangelo, R., and G. Giuliani. 2007. *Special education eligibility: A step-by-step guide for educators*. Thousand Oaks: Corwin Press.

Pierre, R. E. 2008. Beyond textbooks, D.C. schools face a host of social needs. *Washington Post*, March 5.

Sax, L. 2007. *The five factors driving the growing epidemic of unmotivated boys and underachieving men*. New York: Basic Books.

Scholastic Administrator. 2009. RTI demystified: Bolster your program by expanding into middle schools and including more ELL students. Available at http://www.scholastic.com/browse/article.isp?id+3752574.

Shelly, G., T. Cashman, R. Gunter, and G. Gunter. 2008. *Teachers discovering computers: Integrating technology and digital media in the classroom*. 5th ed. Boston: Thomson/Course Technology.

Sirotnik, K. A. 1985. School effectiveness: A bandwagon in search of a tune. *Educational Administration Quarterly* 21 (2): 135–40.

Skinner, E. A., and M. J. Belmont. 1993. Motivation in the classroom: Reciprocal effects of teacher behavior and student engagement across the school year. *Journal of Educational Psychology* 85 (4): 571–81.

Smith, S. 1990. Ninth-grade high school transition course: Building bridges to high school success. Division of Instructional Services, Kent School District, Kent, WA.

Smith, S., K. Curvey-Preston, and E. Woodley. 1991. Expanding the agenda: Building a new system of opportunity for youth. *Curriculum in Context* 21 (2): 26–29.

Smith-Collins, S., and J. E. Collins. 2006. Let the journey begin, destination quality teachers: Is certification a barrier to teaching? Issues, concerns, dilemmas. *Journal of the Alliance of Black School Educators* 5 (2): 20, 24.

Sparks, S. D. 2011. Experts say RtI's use may outrun its research base. *Education Week*, March 2. Retrieved on June 30, 2011, from www.edweek.org/ew/articles/2011.

SpectrumK12 School Solutions. 2010. *Response to intervention (RTI) adoption survey report: Press release and full implementation report*. Retrieved from http://www.spectrumk12.com/rti_survey_results.

Sugai, G., R. H. Horner, and F. M. Gresham. 2002. Behaviorally effective school environments. In *Interventions for academic and behavior problems 2: Preventative and remedial approaches*, ed. M. R. Shinn, G. Stoner, and H. M. Walker, 315–50. Silver Spring, MD: National Association of School Psychologists.

VanDerHeyden, A. M., J. C. Witt, and D. Gilbertson. 2007. A multi-year evaluation of the effects of a response to intervention (RTI) model on identification of children for special education. *Journal of School Psychology* 45:255–56.

Washington State PBIS (Positive Behavioral Interventions and Supports). 2009. School-wide positive behavioral intervention and supports. Seattle: Washington State PBIS. Retrieved from www.wapbis.org.

Weatherly, J. 2008. Districts must ensure that RtI isn't used to block special ed referrals. *Achievement Today* 5. Available at http://www.districtadministration.com/article/districts-must-ensure-rti-isnt-used-block-special-ed-referrals.

Wells, R. H. 2011. Is it time to swap K–12 education trends for common sense solutions? SouthEast Education Network (SEEN). Available at http://www.youthchg.com/seencolumn6.pdf.

About the Author

Searetha Smith-Collins has written books and journal articles that address current educational practices and challenges. Dr. Smith-Collins analyzes educational policies, tools, trends, and innovations and applies her practical experience and educational expertise to translate implications for schools, families, communities, and educators. She has worked in the K–12 educational field as teacher; reading, curriculum, and instruction specialist; principal; program manager; senior administrator; executive director; associate/deputy superintendent; and chief academic officer in several large urban and suburban school districts. Her experience in the educational technology industry has been extensive. She served as vice president and education strategist at SpectrumK12 School Solutions, Inc.; senior education consultant and strategist at Promethean USA, Inc.; manager of strategic initiatives at Apple, Inc.; and vice president of the Syfr Corporation. Currently, Dr. Smith-Collins is president and senior executive consultant at SEA-S Consultants. She is the author of the popular book *The Road to Wisdom, Plain and Simple: Shaping Intelligence, Black Style*. Smith-Collins holds a doctorate degree in policy, governance, and administration and a master's degree in curriculum and instruction from the University of Washington.

Made in the USA
Las Vegas, NV
15 August 2023

76145370R00094